stash happy PATCHWORK

stash happy

PATCHWORK
25 SEWING PROJECTS FOR FABRIC LOVERS

Cynthia Shaffer

LARK CRAFTS

An Imprint of Sterling Publishing Co., Inc.
New York

WWW.LARKCRAFTS.COM

EDITOR: *Amanda Carestio*

ART DIRECTOR: *Megan Kirby*

DESIGNER: *Pamela Norman*

ART ASSISTANT: *Meagan Shirlen*

ILLUSTRATOR: *Susan McBride*

TEMPLATES: *Orrin Lundgren*

PHOTOGRAPHER: *Cynthia Shaffer*

COVER DESIGNER: *Pamela Norman*

Library of Congress Cataloging-in-Publication Data

Shaffer, Cynthia.
  Stash happy : patchwork : 25 sewing projects for fabric lovers / Cynthia Shaffer. -- 1st ed.
    p. cm.
  Includes index.
  ISBN 978-1-60059-612-4
  1. Sewing. 2. Patchwork. 3. Textile fabrics. I. Title.
  TT705.S335 2011
  746.46--dc22

                                2010036282
10 9 8 7 6 5 4 3 2 1

First Edition

Published by Lark Crafts
An Imprint of Sterling Publishing Co., Inc.
387 Park Avenue South, New York, NY 10016

© 2011, Lark Crafts, an Imprint of Sterling Publishing Co., Inc.

Distributed in Canada by Sterling Publishing,
c/o Canadian Manda Group, 165 Dufferin Street
Toronto, Ontario, Canada M6K 3H6

Distributed in the United Kingdom by GMC Distribution Services,
Castle Place, 166 High Street, Lewes, East Sussex, England BN7 1XU

Distributed in Australia by Capricorn Link (Australia) Pty Ltd.,
P.O. Box 704, Windsor, NSW 2756 Australia

If you have questions or comments about this book, please contact:
Lark Crafts
67 Broadway
Asheville, NC 28801
828-253-0467

Manufactured in China

ISBN 13: 978-1-60059-612-4

For information about custom editions, special sales, premium and corporate purchases, please
contact Sterling Special Sales Department at 800-805-5489 or specialsales@sterlingpub.com.

For information about desk and examination copies available to college and university
professors, requests must be submitted to academic@larkbooks.com. Our complete policy
can be found at www.larkcrafts.com.

page 28

page 66

page 63

page 112

stash happy PATCHWORK

online!

Find two free bonus projects at
www.larkcrafts.com/bonus.

Hello fellow stash fiend!

Yummy leftovers too precious to toss, scrappy odds and ends, vintage linens, fabric yardage you fell in love with at first site— if that's what your fabric stash looks like, then you're among friends. Maybe you're saving all that fabric goodness with some- day in mind...Well, hello, someday!

To be sure, there are many stash-collecting styles. If you have a weekly fabric budget, you probably fall into the fabric-a-holic cat- egory. And who can blame you? Those fabulous fabric designers make it so hard with all those delectable patterns...and then you can't help but buy the whole set in each colorway. I feel your pain.

Or perhaps you're more of a fabric scavenger? Vintage sheets and yardage, retro shirts that catch your eye at the thrift store, or whatever's in the linen closet (or fresh from the dryer, for that matter)—there's not a moment when you're not feeling opportu- nistic about fabric.

No matter your approach, I feel like a healthy stash makes for a happy crafter. And I've created a collection of projects to feature your favorite fabrics, make the most of your scraps (it's okay if you can't let them go!), and offer fun ways to upcycle things you've never considered part of your stash before.

And what better way to flaunt your fabric stash than with patchwork projects? From the littlest bits to larger scraps to fun strips, patchwork is perfect! Try traditional blocks and patterns— hexagons, Dresden plates, and broken dish blocks, all used in inventive ways—or go the improv route with freeform log cabins and plus signs.

All 25 projects are fresh, fun, and waiting for your personal spin...and your favorite fabrics.

- *Spice up your fabulously organized (or "inspiringly messy") creative space: Make a too-cute cactus pincushion (page 36) or a neat-as-a-button travel sewing kit (page 94).*
- *Dress your nest with patchwork upholstery (page 18) or a delightful Dresden plate rug (page 86).*
- *Decorate...your children (or someone else's!) with a diamond- pieced vest (page 102) and a little pieced dress (page 14), great starter projects if you're new to garment sewing.*

So get crafty with your stash...and get stash happy!

basics

gather

Seems like we crafty types have the "gather" thing down pat. And that's definitely part of the fun: seeing potential in random scraps others might toss, taking the plunge when a good fabric deal presents itself, or holding on to a pretty pillowcase for a pretty something down the road. You'll need a few items, in addition to fabulous fabric, to make these patchwork projects. See the tool kit on page 7.

Stash, Glorious, Stash!

If you've already assembled a legiti- mate fabric stash, chances are you know everything you need to know about fabric (and maybe too much!). But any way you slice it, stash is a pretty glorious thing. Even better, this collection of projects will encour- age you to look at your own collection in a sparkling new way, and maybe expand your own notions of "stash."

make

Once you've gathered up all those handy bits, you're ready to get to work. If you need it, here's a little refresher on cutting and using templates and then some more involved techniques.

Using Templates

In the back of the book, you'll find all of the templates you need to make the projects. Enlarge the templates based on the percentages listed and then follow the individual project instructions for using them. You can also use the templates as inspiration points for your own creative re-interpretation of the designs. All of which you'll need to do before…

Cutting Up

Before you cut into your store of lovely fabric (and especially if you're a bit nervous about doing so), be sure to wash the fabrics first and give them a quick press if needed. If you're using scraps from other projects, chances are you've already completed this step.

Once your fabric is prepped and ready, you can cut into it using the project instructions as a guide. Most of these projects involve cutting with a rotary system to create nice, neat shapes—like squares and strips—for patchwork piecing. Or cut freestyle "wonky" shapes (i.e., perfectly imperfect) if that's more your style. When it comes to patchwork, the rotary cutter is your friend and ally.

For other more involved shapes, you'll need to cut various pattern pieces (usually with a pair of nice, sharp sewing scissors) using the templates provided. Sometimes, if there's a bit of a special patterned fabric that you want to highlight, you may need to do what is called "fussy" cutting. But rest assured: The process isn't fussy at all! You simply cut around the pattern in the fabric so the shape you want is featured in the bit you use for piecing.

patchwork tool kit

* Sewing machine
* Rotary cutter + mat
* Measuring tape + ruler
* Scissors
* Straight pins
* Hand-sewing needles
* Iron + ironing board
* Embroidery needle + hoop
* Washable fabric marker or sharp pencil
* Other nice-to-have items include a sharp pointy utensil (for turning), pincushions, + floss organizers.

You'll also need a few more standard supplies like spray adhesive, stuffing, muslin, and batting. And, of course, a handy system for organizing your stash so it's nice + neat, always within reach, and visible enough so you don't forget you have it— but not in an overwhelming guilt-inducing way.

PLUNDERING YOUR *stash*

In these projects, I've used all kinds of stash:

LOVELY COTTON PRINTS (of course) Old standbys never looked so good!

ITTY BITTY SCRAPS Cupcake flags anyone? See page 98.

FLANNEL The Scrappy Scoodie on page 74 uses yardage, but you could definitely use a couple of old shirts instead.

OLD LINENS Pillowcases create the perfect kitchen palette for the Retro Apron on page 66.

IMPULSE BIG-YARDAGE BUYS Turn that shopper's guilt into a cute Patchy Wrap Skirt on page 41.

And don't forget embroidery floss, ribbons, buttons, piping, fun trims, binding/bias tape, and, of course, thread. I think all of that counts as stash, too, and I encourage collecting, since notions are perfect for adding that extra special something to a handmade project.

Piecing

Okay, now we get into the meaty part of the patchwork process: the piecing. Most of the piecing for the projects in this book happens on a machine, but feel free to experiment with hand stitching. The basic piecing process couldn't be easier: Essentially, you pin one piece of fabric to another with right sides facing **(fig. A)**, run them through your sewing machine **(fig. B)**, and then press the seams flat **(fig. C)**, either both to one side or open. There are, of course, lots of variations of that theme—especially when it comes to creating some of the more involved blocks—but you get the drift.

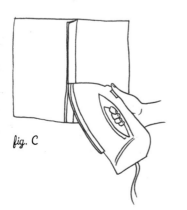

fig. A

fig. B

fig. C

chain reaction

When it comes to simple piecework, knowing a few tricks can really save you some time. Chaining is one of those tricks. With this simple technique, you can move through a whole stack of piecing rather quickly: Simply feed your pieces through the machine one after another, leaving a little space between them. When you're done, you'll have a little "chain" of pieced bits. Cut them apart, and you're ready for the next step.

For the more involved blocks used in particular projects, the instructions include information both for cutting and for the piecing order. But don't worry: Even for the more intricate blocks, it's still only a matter of stitching an edge of one piece to the edge of another.

One thing to keep in mind while you're piecing things together is the seam allowance. This is a pretty standard thing in all sewing and quilting instructions, and the simple definition is, well, quite simple: Seam allowance is the space between your stitched line and the raw edge of the fabric. The throat plate on most sewing machines indicates this measurement. The standard seam allowance for the projects in this book is $1/4$ inch (6 mm) unless otherwise noted.

English Paper Piecing

Some piecing requires a slightly more careful hand because some shapes get their charm from their perfect corners and angles. Hexagons, like the kind on the Honeycomb Sheet Set (page 28), wouldn't have their same appeal if they weren't perfect, and to get that perfect shape, English paper piecing is the way to go.

The basic process is this: Cut paper templates for the number of shapes you'll be creating. Use the templates to cut fabric shapes, adding a $1/4$-inch (6 mm) seam allowance **(fig. D)**. Press the fabric seam allowance over the edge of the paper **(fig. E)**. Pin the paper template to the fabric shape and baste the corners and edges **(fig. F)**. Continue working to prepare all of your shapes. Use a ladder stitch (as shown), appliqué stitch, or slip-stitch to attach the pieces together as close to the edge as possible and then remove the basting stitches and the paper **(fig. G)**.

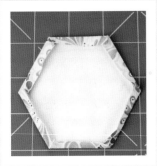

fig. D

fig. E

fig. F

fig. G

Piecing Strips

Strips of fabric are my favorite kind of scrap: You can do so much with them. And there are lots of shortcuts for working with strips, which is sometimes called strip piecing. For example, to make the apron for the Pretty Petite Dress (page 14), I first pieced a group of strips together **(fig. H)**, cut those pieced strips into strips **(fig. I)**, and stitched the strips together again **(fig. J)**, all of which took way less time than piecing little 1-inch (2.5 cm) square blocks together. And, oh, the possibilities for wonkiness with strips, which brings us to…

Free-form Piecing

Free-form—or improv—piecing applies to the process of cutting and stitching your patchwork pieces together without perfection in mind. It's a process, really, and it can lend a certain spirit and style to your work. The Log Cabin Bucket project (page 78) was pieced in this way, with log cabins as the basic structure of the block. This process usually involves starting with free-form cut pieces, stitching the pieces together **(fig. K)**, and then trimming the final shape flush—or with perfect 90° angles—before assembly **(fig. L)**. Free-form is a great process to pick when you want to riff off a traditional block pattern for something that is less structured or when you're piecing together strips of fabric to create a bigger fabric with which to work.

fig. H

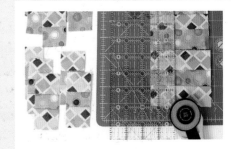

fig. I

fig. J

fig. K

fig. L

Stitching

For most of the projects in this collection, I've combined patchwork with all kinds of yummy stitching, which you'll do before final assembly and finishing steps. I love this part of the process! There are a few basic machine stitches and terms you should be familiar with.

Basting Stitch: Perfect for when you need to hold something in place temporarily, create a basting stitch using a long stitch length on your machine. You can also create this stitch by hand by sewing a long running stitch.

Gathering Stitch: Very similar to the basting stitch, the gathering stitch is created using a long stitch length on your machine. The standard process is to create two lines of a long running stitch about $1/4$ inch (6 mm) apart. Pull the threads to create ruffles evenly along the line of stitching. Create a regular line of stitching in between the first two stitch lines to secure the ruffles in place.

Topstitch: Sometimes functional and sometimes simply decorative, there's nothing fancy about this term—simply stitch with the top facing up.

Zigzag Stitch: If you're planning on doing machine appliqué or anything with a raw edge exposed, the zigzag stitch is your friend. When done over the edge of fabric, it can reduce fraying.

Quilting

Many of the projects in this book involve creating a top layer of patchwork that is layered together with batting (or nonwoven interfacing, as in the Bento Box and the Sew on the Go Kit) and a backing layer and then stitching through the layers, as you would do when making a traditional quilt. When you're stitching through the layers, you've got some options.

Stitch in the Ditch: In this process, you stitch into the seams created by your patchwork process, meaning your stitch lines are virtually invisible.

Straight-Stitch Quilting: The name says it all: For this technique, you create straight lines of quilting. You can also create evenly spaced lines of quilting—often with a quilting bar attachment—for a simple linear design with strong stitch lines **(fig. M).**

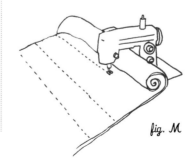

fig. M

Free Motion: For free-motion stitching, you drop your feed dogs, attach a quilting or darning foot, and guide the fabric through your sewing machine to create a free-form stitch line. A common method is to create a continuous, meandering line of stitches called stippling **(fig N).**

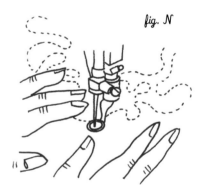

fig. N

Tying: Although I haven't used any ties in these projects, ties are a design option—and they're so simple. With wool yarn, perle cotton, or embroidery floss, you simply stitch down through the layers, come back up, and then tie the loose ends together.

Embroidery & Hand Stitches

Oh, embroidered goodness, how I love thee! I've used a variety of hand stitches in these projects, some of which serve a useful purpose (like the blind stitch) and some of which just look pretty. To the right is a handy chart with all the stitches you'll need to know for the projects in this book.

Appliqué

In a few projects, appliqué adds an additional layer of design interest and cuteness! And when it comes to appliqué, I'm a big fan of spray adhesive. I simply cut out my appliqué shape, spray the back of it, position it on my fabric, and stitch it in place. No more shifting fabric and pokes from pins. And with temporary fabric spray (the kind I use), you can even reposition the shape if it's not right the first time. Keep in mind that this kind of adhesive will wash out, so you'll need to stitch your shape in place firmly.

The stitching you do is up to you: You can create a simple stitched line (leaving the edges raw), zigzag stitch over the edge, or create a decorative embroidery stitch—like a blanket stitch—over the edges. If you'd like your appliqué edges to be nice and neat, you may opt for turning the edges of your appliqué shapes under and then using a blind (or hidden) stitch, which is basically invisible.

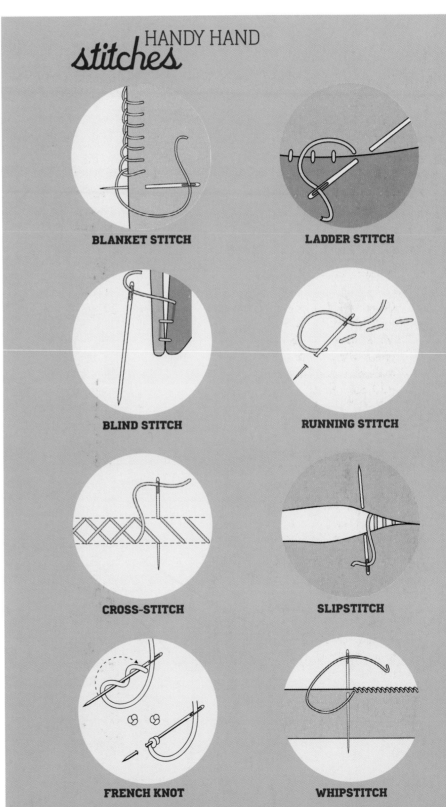

HANDY HAND
stitches

BLANKET STITCH

LADDER STITCH

BLIND STITCH

RUNNING STITCH

CROSS-STITCH

SLIPSTITCH

FRENCH KNOT

WHIPSTITCH

Assembly & Finishing

You're well on your way to patchwork goodness...just a few more steps and your project will be ready to flaunt, use, or give.

Binding

Binding serves a functional purpose and, let's face it, it adds that perfect pretty edge to patchwork items including many in this book. Here are the basic steps, and I'll share a few tips I use along the way.

Making Your Own Binding

Binding is available in stores, but as long as you're going to all that trouble for that perfect handmade something, you might as well create your own.

❶ To determine the total length of the binding you'll need, add together the lengths of the edges you're binding, plus a little extra for safety.

❷ Cut a strip of fabric to the recommended width in the project instructions.

If you need to connect strips together to make one long strip, you can pin and stitch the short ends of your strips together **(fig. O)**, with the right sides facing, until you have one long strip, and then press the seams open.

Or you can pin the short ends of your strips together at a right angle, with right sides facing, and stitch diagonally across the corner **(fig. P)**. Trim the seam allowance, press the seams open, and bind away.

fig. O

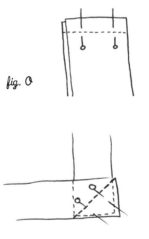

fig. P

Binding with Mitered Corners

Single binding is my favorite way to finish my patchwork projects. I sometimes use double-layer binding, but the basic steps are pretty much the same.

❶ After you've quilted the layers together, lay your project flat and trim the layers so they're all the same size.

❷ Starting midway on one edge or near a corner, pin and then stitch the right side of the binding to the right side of the fabric **(fig. Q)**, folding over the starting edge. Use the seam allowance in the instructions.

❸ Stop stitching as you approach the first corner and clip the threads to remove the project from the machine. Fold the binding straight up over itself to form a 45° angle at the corner **(fig. R)**.

❹ Fold the binding straight down to make it even with the next edge and continue pinning and stitching the binding in place **(fig. S)**. Continue working your way around the edges, using the same process for any additional corners.

❺ When you near your starting point, stitch your binding strip over the folded-over starting edge of the binding.

❻ Fold the binding over the edges (not too tightly) to the back. Turn under the raw edge just enough to cover the seam that you just stitched. Place the prepared edge just barely over the seam line that attached the binding and pin it down along the edges. Create diagonal folds at the corners and pin them in place.

❼ Working from the back, use a slip-stitch to attach the binding **(fig. T)**. Working from the front, stitch in the ditch.

washing a quilted project

Some quilted items get a soft, worn-in feel after the first washing that can really add to the overall personality of the project. This is especially true for the French Bistro Set and for free-motion-stitched things. Think Wonky Cottage Lap Quilt... only cozier!

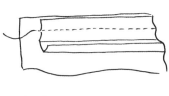

fig. Q

fig. R

fig. S

fig. T

A WORD ABOUT *wonky*

"Wonky" is just one of the given terms (although it happens to be my favorite) to the end product of free-form or improvisational piecing. Now, how you feel about wonky is totally up to you. Many modern quilters and patchworkers find wonky appealing. Some folks are simply drawn to the aesthetic, some enjoy the freestyle nature and lack of rules (although there are still many of those), and some like the shift of focus from a perfect creation to an improvisational creative process. However, good wonky can be hard to achieve. It takes a little confidence at times, too, but the results can be freeing.

However, there are plenty of merits in perfect patchwork. Most every crafter would agree that you have to know the rules before you break them. Striving for perfection can be a good way to train and teach yourself, especially if you're just starting out. And some folks just like the clean, neat, and tidy aesthetic better.

LOG CABIN BUCKET
This bucket's imperfect log cabins are totally charming.

BENTO BOX
This lunch bag gains its appeal, in part, from its clean and perfect lines.

WONKY COTTAGE LAP QUILT
These little cottages are cute in their imperfections, but a nice, neat neighborhood of houses would also be lovely.

SEW ON THE GO KIT
The free-pieced sides of the kit offer a nice balance to the geometric shape of the whole.

It's really a matter of preference. If I've made something wonky that you'd rather see clean and neat, go for that. If our perfect lines and corners aren't exciting to you, wonk-ify to your heart's content.

A pretty dress—in miniature—makes for
a darling decoration to hang anywhere.

pretty PETITE DRESS

from your stash

1 piece of fabric for dress,
15 x 15 inches (38.1 x 38.1 cm)

Fabric scraps (for apron, collar,
and trim)

1 piece of backing fabric,
15 x 15 inches (38.1 x 38.1 cm)

gather

Basic sewing tool kit (page 7)

Templates (page 123)

1 piece of batting, 15 x 15 inches
(38.1 x 38.1 cm)

Embroidery floss

3 flat buttons

make

the dress

❶ Using template A, cut the following pieces: one dress with primary fabric,
one dress with batting, and one dress with backing fabric. Using template B,
cut two collar self pieces and two collar lining pieces.

❷ With stash fabric, cut two armband pieces that measure $2^1/_2$ x 1 inch
(6.4 x 2.5 cm) and one belt piece that measures 7 x 1 inch (17.8 x 2.5 cm).

❸ Pin all the dress layers together, and free-motion quilt the bodice. Quilt
vertical lines in the skirt. Machine stitch together all the layers around the
perimeter.

❹ Create two small tucks at each sleeve for a sleeve width of $2^1/_2$ inches
(6.4 cm). Pin and then stitch in place **(fig. A)**.

❺ Press the armbands in half lengthwise, encase the sleeve edges, and stitch
in place.

fig. A

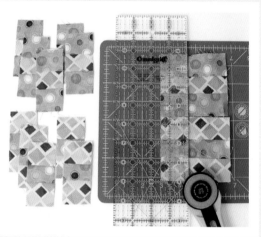

fig. B

fig. C

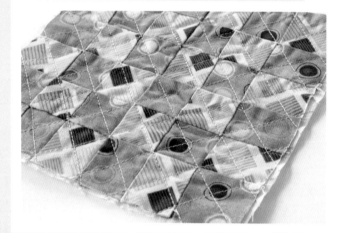

fig. D

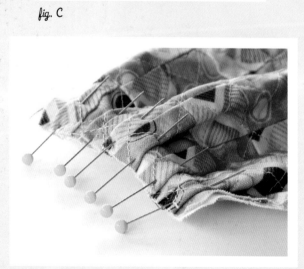

fig. E

fig. F

the apron

6 Using two coordinating fabrics (fabric A and fabric B), cut three strips of each fabric that measure 1½ x 13 inches (3.8 x 33 cm), for a total of six strips.

7 Create two wide strips. With right sides together, sew one strip of fabric A to one strip of fabric B. Sew another strip of fabric A to finish sewing one wide strip. With right sides together, sew one strip of fabric B to the remaining strip of fabric A. Sew the remaining strip of fabric B to finish sewing the second wide strip.

TIP

Press the seams in the first wide strip inward, and press the seams in the second wide strip outward. This will ease the piecing of the apron top.

8 Stack the strips onto a cutting mat and cut twelve 1½-inch-long (3.8 cm) segments with a rotary cutter and quilter's ruler **(fig. B)**.

9 Organize the cut segments into four large squares, placing fabrics A and B in a rotating sequence. With right sides together, sew the segments together **(fig. C)**. Then, sew the four squares together.

10 Cut a piece of backing fabric that measures approximately ¼ inch (6 mm) wider and longer than the patchwork apron. Pin together the apron top and backing fabric.

11 Machine quilt diagonally from corner to corner to create a diamond motif **(fig. D)**. Trim away the backing fabric and hand quilt around the edge with a large running stitch and embroidery floss.

12 Cut a piece of stash fabric slightly larger than the apron. Baste the fabric to the top edge of the apron.

13 Hand tuck pleats at the top of the apron for an apron width 3½ inches (8.9 cm) smaller than the waist of the dress. Pin in place and stitch **(fig. E)**.

14 Fold the belt piece in half lengthwise. Encase the top edge of the apron, and stitch in place **(fig. F)**.

finishing

15 Wrap the apron belt around the dress and hand stitch in place at the back.

16 Layer the self and lining pieces for the collars, and stitch around the perimeter edges. Stitch the collars onto the dress.

17 Embellish the dress with buttons to finish **(fig. G)**.

fig. G

variation!
Using the dress as a door decoration? Stitch a name or piece initials into the apron.

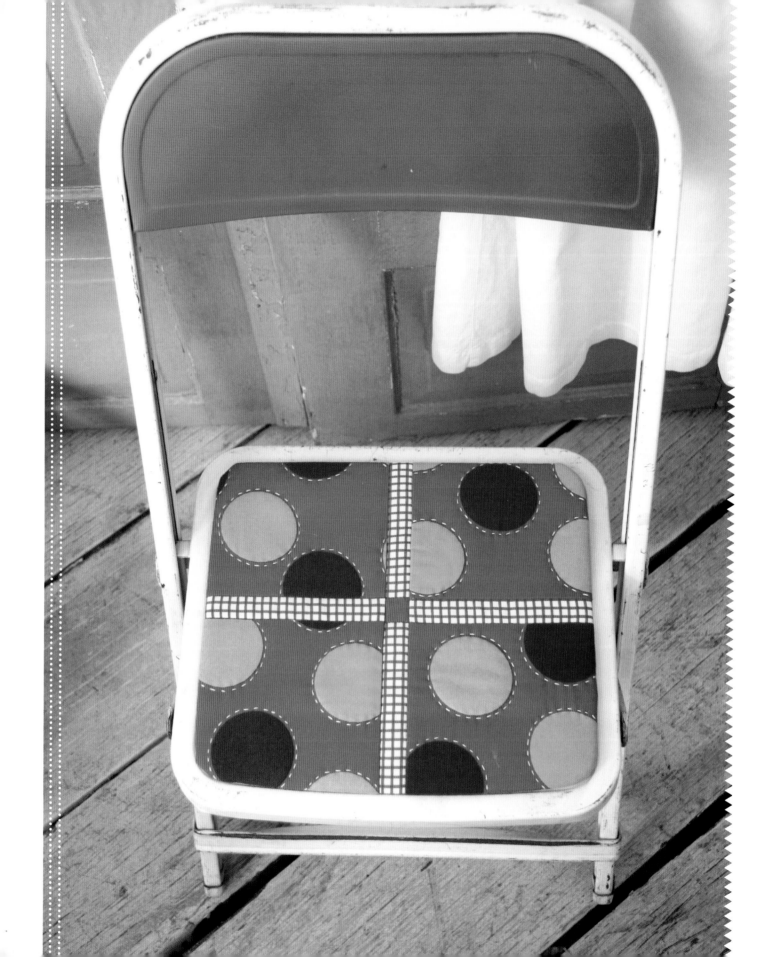

hit-the-deck CHAIR

Patchwork upholstery? Yes, please! This folding deck chair makes for the perfect weekend upcycle project.

from your stash

¹/₃ yard (.3 m) of fabric (primary color)

¹/₄ yard (.2 m) of fabric (two coordinating colors)

¹/₃ yard (.3 m) of backing fabric

gather

Basic sewing tool kit (page 7)

Folding chair with removable seat base

1 piece of batting, 14 x 14 inches (35.6 x 35.6 cm)

Embroidery floss

Glue, staples, or upholstery tacks

note: Fabric amounts are approximate. See step 2 to calculate how much fabric you'll need.

make

❶ Remove and discard the chair's existing seat cover.

❷ Measure the seat base, and add approximately 4 inches (10.2 cm) to the height and width to account for seam allowances, quilting, and folding the fabric over the seat base.

❸ Select the primary fabric and cut it to the calculated measurement. Then, cut this fabric piece horizontally and vertically through the center **(fig. A)**.

❹ With a coordinating fabric, cut one strip that measures 1¹/₄ inches (3.2 cm) by the total length of the piece you cut in step 3 and one strip that is 1¹/₄ inches (3.2 cm) by the total width. Then, cut these strips in half. You will have four strips.

❺ From your primary fabric, cut a square that measures 1¹/₄ x 1¹/₄ inches (3.2 x 3.2 cm).

❻ Lay out the squares and strips of fabric in a grid so that the strips separate each square of primary fabric. Place the small square of primary fabric at the center. Use the laid out pieces as a guide as you assemble the pieces. With right sides together, sew the top left piece of fabric to the top vertical strip of coordinating fabric. Repeat in like fashion to sew the top right piece of fabric to the top vertical strip **(fig. B)**.

fig. A

fig. B

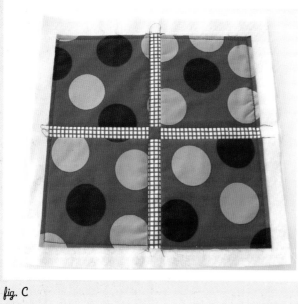

fig. C

fig. D

7 With right sides together, sew the left horizontal strip to the center square. Repeat in like fashion to sew the right horizontal strip to the center square.

8 With right sides together, sew the bottom left piece of fabric to the bottom vertical strip of coordinating fabric. Repeat in like fashion to sew the bottom right piece of fabric to the bottom vertical strip.

9 With right sides facing, sew together the sections from steps 6, 7, and 8 to finish the patchwork piece.

10 Cut the batting and backing fabric so that each measures approximately 2 inches (5.1 cm) longer and wider than the patchwork piece. Pin the quilt top, batting, and backing layers together.

11 Stitch in the ditch, where all the patchwork pieces meet. Stitch around the perimeter of the entire piece **(fig. C)**.

12 Using a large running stitch, hand stitch around the circles or other pattern motif of the primary fabric using embroidery floss **(fig. D)**.

13 Fold the sides of the patchwork panel over the seat base and secure it with glue, staples, or upholstery tacks. This final step will vary, depending on the type of chair you select for this project.

panda BOLSTER

Thanks to chain stitching and easy-peasy broken dish blocks, this playful panda is as fast to make as he is fun to squeeze.

from your stash

¹/₄ yard (.2 m) of white fabrics (for quilt blocks and end pieces)

Fabrics scraps (for quilt blocks)

¹/₈ yard (.1 m) of black fabrics

gather

Basic sewing tool kit (page 7)

Templates (page 123)

¹/₃ yard (.3 m) of muslin

Polyester fiberfill

Embroidery floss

2 buttons and 1 snap, or other embellishments

make

broken dish blocks

1 Select two white fabrics. Cut the fabrics into 2-inch-wide (5.1 cm) strips. Cut the strips from each fabric into 14 squares that measure 2 x 2 inches (5.1 x 5.1 cm), for a total of 28 white fabric squares.

2 Select six patterned fabrics and repeat step 1 in like fashion for a total of 28 patterned squares. Four of the fabrics should yield four squares each, and two of the fabrics should yield six squares each.

3 Cut each square diagonally into half-square triangles **(fig. A)**.

4 Pair each white fabric triangle with a patterned fabric triangle, and align them, right sides together. Stitch each pair together at the longest sides of the triangles, chain piecing to save time. When you finish, you will have 56 squares made up of white and patterned triangle pairs.

5 Gather four stitched squares of one fabric pattern. Using the photo as a guide, position the four squares and press the seams toward the dark fabric. Next, stitch the top squares together and press the seam to the left **(fig. B)**. Finally, stitch together the top and bottom segments so the seam allowances lock in place. This completes one Broken Dish Block **(fig. C)**.

6 Repeat the process in step 5 to create 14 Broken Dish Blocks.

fig. A

fig. B

fig. C

fig. D

fig. E

fig. F

the body

7 With a white fabric, cut a strip that measures $2^{7}/_{8}$ x 40 inches (7.3 x 101.6 cm). Cut this strip into 13 squares that measure $2^{7}/_{8}$ x $2^{7}/_{8}$ inches (7.3 x 7.3 cm).

8 Alternate these squares with the Broken Dish Blocks to create three rows with nine blocks total in each row. Be strategic as you position the squares so that a diagonal pattern emerges. Play around with an occasional Broken Dish Block or two, rotating them to create unexpected patterns as desired **(fig. D)**.

9 Stitch the bottom row of blocks and squares together. Press all seams toward the solid white squares. Repeat in like fashion with the middle and upper rows.

10 Stitch the bottom and middle rows together so that the seam allowances lock in place. Repeat in like fashion with the top row.

11 Select two black fabrics. Cut a strip from each fabric that measures $2^{1}/_{2}$ x $21^{3}/_{4}$ inches (6.4 x 55.2 cm). Stitch a black strip to each long side of the patchwork panel **(fig. E)**.

12 Lay the entire piece on top of a large piece of muslin. Trim the muslin so that it is slightly larger than the patchwork piece, and pin the layers together. Machine quilt diagonally through the Broken Dish patterns. Then, quilt horizontally across all three rows **(fig. F)**.

13 Stitch along the entire perimeter and trim the excess muslin.

14 With right sides together, bring the short ends of the quilted panel together and stitch, leaving a 6-inch (15.2 cm) opening in the middle. This opening will allow the panda to be stuffed with polyester fiberfill.

the circular ends of the body

15 Using the panda ends template pattern and two white fabrics, cut eight segments of fabric. Stitch the segments together to create four half circles. Then, stitch the half circles together to create two full circles.

16 Using the circles as templates, cut a piece of muslin for each, slightly larger than the circles.

17 Lay the pieced circles on top of the muslin circles. Stitch in the ditch along the seams and quilt diagonally twice across each circle.

the limbs

18 From coordinating black fabrics, cut four pieces using the ear template and eight pieces using the leg template. With right sides together, pair up the ear and leg pieces, and stitch each pair together, leaving the short edge unstitched.

19 Clip V-shaped notches into the curve of each stitched piece, and turn right side out. Use polyester fiberfill to lightly stuff each ear and leg.

20 Position the front legs $2^{1}/_{2}$ inches (6.4 cm) apart, near the center underbelly. Pin and stitch in place. Repeat in like fashion with the back legs **(fig. G)**.

21 Position the ears on the edge of the body at the top so that they are $4^{1}/_{4}$ inches (10.8 cm) apart. Pin and stitch in place.

fig. G

fig. H

fig. J

fig. I

fig. K

finishing

22 Turn the body inside out and position one of the quilted circles so that the top seam of the circle meets the top back of the body and the opposite circular seam meets the underbelly seam. Pin and stitch in place. Repeat in like fashion with the remaining quilted circle at the other end of the body **(fig. H)**.

23 Using the opening at the underbelly, turn the body right side out.

24 Using embroidery floss, add a large running stitch on both sides of one of the black strips **(fig. I)**. When stitching, make sure that the seam allowances on both sides of the strip lay flat toward the black strip. Repeat in like fashion to add running stitches on the other black strip.

25 Stuff the panda with polyester fiberfill. Close the opening at the underbelly with a whipstitch.

26 To make the tail, cut a circle with a 3½-inch (8.9 cm) diameter from black fabric.

27 Using a needle and thread, sew a basting stitch around the outer edge of the circle. Draw up the thread, and stuff the circle with polyester fiberfill. Stitch back and forth to securely close the circle.

28 Attach the stuffed circle to the rear of the panda to create its tail **(fig. J)**.

29 Add the buttons, the snap, and embroidery to create the panda's eyes, nose, and mouth **(fig. K)**.

variation!

Not a panda person? Adjust the ear and tail shapes to make a pink pig, a long dachshund, or a striped tiger bolster instead.

honeycomb SHEET SET

Pick colors that match your bedroom for this fresh hexagon-patterned linen set. Wouldn't these look too sweet under a hexagon quilt?

from your stash

²/₃ yard (.6 m) of assorted fabrics

gather

Basic sewing tool kit (page 7)

Templates (page 121)

Cardstock (1 sheet) and standard office paper

Water-soluble ink pen

1 pillowcase and flat sheet

make

1 Cut out template A from cardstock.

2 Using template B and office paper, cut approximately 26 paper templates.

3 With a water-soluble ink pen, trace the cardstock template A on your assorted fabrics 26 times. Cut out the shapes. Place the template strategically on fabrics with large patterns so that you can fussy cut and capture specific parts of the pattern (**fig. A**).

4 Center one office paper template B onto a piece of cut fabric, and fold the sides of the fabric over the edges of the paper. Sew a basting stitch around the perimeter of the fabric, going through the paper. Repeat in like fashion with all 26 fabric pieces and office paper templates (**fig. B**).

fig. A

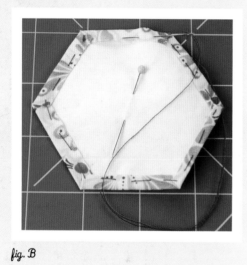

fig. B

fig. C

fig. D

fig. E

5 Line up the hexagons as desired and piece them together using a ladder stitch **(fig. C)**.

6 Pin the patchwork hexagons to the pillowcase as desired **(fig. D)**. Stitch in place using a blind stitch. During this process, leave one side of each hexagon unstitched, so that you can remove the basting stitches and the office paper. After removing the stitches and paper, use a blind stitch to secure the final side of each hexagon **(fig. E)**.

7 Repeat these same steps to make the coordinating sheet.

variation!

Hexagons look cute everywhere! Add them to a plain shower curtain, standard throw pillows, or the bottom edge of kitchen bistro curtains for a pleasant pop of color.

cozy CONES

During the holidays or any time of year, these cones are just the thing for holding treats and goodies.

from your stash

2 squares of fabric (two coordinating colors), 10 x 10 inches (25.4 x 25.4 cm)

Fabric scrap for the rosette

gather

Basic sewing tool kit (page 7)

Template (page 122)

$^1/_3$ yard (.3 m) of batting

Embroidery floss or perle cotton

1 flat button and other embellishments (optional)

13 inches (33 cm) of wire

Ribbon

make

the cone

1 Using the template and the coordinating fabric squares, cut a top, middle, and bottom portion of the cone **(fig. A)**.

2 Stitch the portions together.

3 Using the patchwork cone shapes as a template, cut out a piece of batting with an extra $^1/_4$ inch (6 mm) at the top curve. Layer the batting with the stitched cone piece.

4 Machine quilt as desired, and stitch around the perimeter edges. Embroider accents with embroidery floss **(fig. B)**.

5 Overlap the edges of the cone by $2^1/_2$ inches (6.4 cm), and hand stitch them in place using a running stitch **(fig. C)**.

fig. A

fig. B

fig. C

fig. D

fig. E

fig. F

the rosette

6 Cut a piece of fabric that measures 1 x 7 inches (2.5 x 17.8 cm).

7 Sew a running stitch along one lengthwise edge, gather up, and secure **(fig. D, fig. E)**.

8 Stitch the flat button to the center of the rosette, and attach the rosette as desired onto the cone. Add additional embellishments if desired.

finishing

9 To add a handle, poke the ends of the wire through the top side edges of the cone. Bend the wire to secure. Add a ribbon to finish **(fig. F)**.

variation!

Use the same techniques, with varying embellishments and quilting motifs, to create different variations of the cone.

cactus PINCUSHION

This prickly pincushion doesn't need a drop of water—just small scraps of green fabric from your stash.

from your stash

Green fabric scraps, assorted

Red fabric scraps, assorted

gather

Basic sewing tool kit (page 7)

Templates (page 123)

Embroidery floss

Polyester fiberfill

Circular container, such as a bucket or small bowl

Hot glue or strong-hold adhesive

make

the main body

1 Using the templates and coordinating green fabrics, cut the pieces needed to construct the three sides that make up the main body of the cactus. Snip the notches with scissors before you remove the template patterns.

2 With right sides together, pin the top and bottom portions of each side and sew.

3 Press each seam to one side, and use embroidery floss to add a running stitch close to each seam.

4 With right sides together, pin two sections together along one side, matching the top center notches. Starting from the notches, sew to the bottom edge.

5 With right sides together, pin the third section to both sides of the work-in-progress, matching the top center notches. Starting from the notches, sew to the bottom edge to join the pieces together **(fig. A)**.

fig. A

fig. B

fig. D

fig. C

fig. E

6 Cut small snips on the uppermost curved sections. These snips will allow the curved seam to lie smooth when turned right side out.

TIP
To speed up this process, fold the sewn edge and cut once at an angle, creating a small triangular snip in one step.

7 Turn the work. Use embroidery floss to add a running stitch close to the seams **(fig. B)** and stuff with polyester fiberfill.

8 Fold under the raw edges of the body and pin them in place. Baste with a large running stitch. Remove pins.

the arms

9 Using the template patterns and co-ordinating green fabrics, cut the pieces needed to construct the two arms of the cactus. Snip the notches with scissors and create dart placement marks with a washable marker or pencil before you remove the template patterns. The template will yield one center and two side pieces for each arm.

10 With right sides together, pin one side piece to a center piece, matching the top center notches. Starting from the notches, sew to the bottom edge. Repeat this step to sew a second side piece to the center section.

11 Fold the work-in-progress along the dart fold line. Pin and sew in place **(fig. C)**.

12 Sew the two side pieces together with right sides facing. This step will feel counterintuitive because of the curve created by the dart **(fig. D)**.

13 Repeat steps 9 through 12 to make the second arm.

14 Cut small snips on the uppermost curved sections of both arms. Turn the arms right side out and stuff them with polyester fiberfill.

15 Fold under the raw edges of the arms and pin them in place. Baste with a large running stitch to keep these edges folded under. Remove pins.

16 Pin the arms in place as desired on the cactus. Using a blind stitch, attach the arms in place **(fig. E)**.

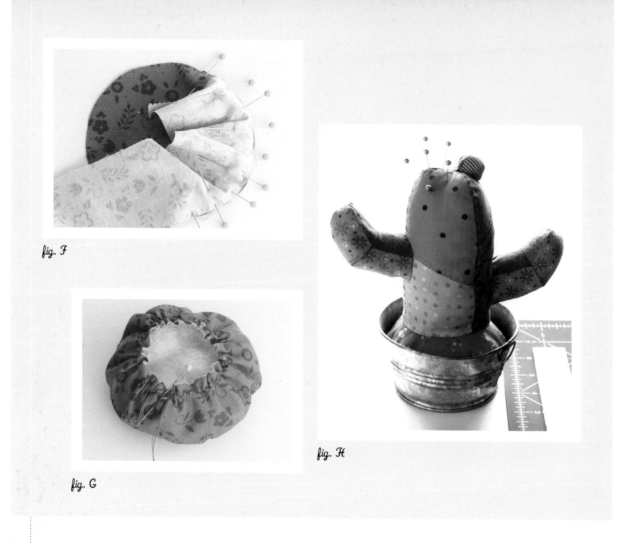

fig. F

fig. G

fig. H

the base & finishing

17 Using the largest opening of the circular container as a template and your red fabric, cut a circle of fabric for the base.

18 Using the same fabric, cut a strip long enough to go around the circle, plus an extra $^3/_4$ inch (1.9 cm) for overlap. Determine the strip's width by measuring the height of the base minus $^1/_4$ inch (6 mm).

19 Pin the strip along the curved edge and sew **(fig. F)**.

20 Run a machine gathering stitch along the outer edge of the strip. Stuff with fiberfill and draw up the gathering stitch and secure in place **(fig. G)**.

21 Pin the cactus onto the fabric base and attach with a blind stitch.

22 Cut a circle of red fabric with a $2^1/_2$-inch (6.4 cm) diameter. Run a machine gathering stitch along the outer edge of the circle. Stuff with polyester fiberfill and draw up the gathering stitch. Tie the ends. Pin the stuffed circle to the top of the cactus and attach it with a blind stitch.

23 Use hot glue or other strong-hold adhesive to attach the entire pincushion to the container **(fig. H)**.

variation!

Plant your cactus in a soufflé cup. Or use the basic design to make other plant-like creations, perfect for pins or as cheery decoration around your home (especially if you have trouble keeping house plants alive).

patchy WRAP SKIRT

Inside-out or outside-in, this skirt always looks fresh and pretty thanks to a handful of coordinating fabrics and a reversible design.

from your stash

1½ yards (1.4 m) of primary fabric (three coordinating colors)

1½ yards (1.4 m) of secondary fabric (three coordinating colors)

Fabric scraps (leftover primary fabric)

gather

Basic sewing tool kit (page 7)

Template (page 122)

Scrap of batting

note: finished skirt length is 16 inches (40.6 cm).

make

before you get started

- Use a ¼-inch (6 mm) seam allowance for all seams.
- Enlarge the template and determine how many skirt segments you will need to create a skirt that fits you. Add three extra skirt segments for overlap. (I recommend that you print out several templates at one time.) The size of the skirt can be adjusted by adding or reducing the number of the template segments. The skirt instructions below use 10 segments in three coordinating fabrics for the primary side and three coordinating fabrics for the reverse side.

- The template has a cut line. Be sure to cut the template at that line for the outer skirt. Pin the top portion of the template onto the fabric first, and then pin the bottom portion of the template at least ½ inch (1.3 cm) below the top portion. This space allows you to add a ¼-inch (6 mm) seam allowance to both the top and bottom portions before cutting the fabric.
- After you determine how many segments you need, I suggest creating a "practice" skirt with plain muslin before you dive into your fabric stash to create the final skirt.

IT'S REVERSIBLE!

fig. A

fig. B

the primary side

1 With two of the coordinating fabrics, cut three sets of the template pattern (top and bottom, including seam allowances). With the third coordinating fabric, cut four sets of the template pattern (top and bottom, including seam allowances).

2 With right sides together, pin and stitch the top and bottom portions of the cut fabrics, mixing and matching fabrics **(fig. A)**.

TIP
Chain piece these segments to save time.

3 Press the seams toward the lower portions of the segments.

4 Matching the lower seams together, stitch all of the segments together. Press the vertical seams open **(fig. B)**.

5 Topstitch along the bottom segments of the skirt.

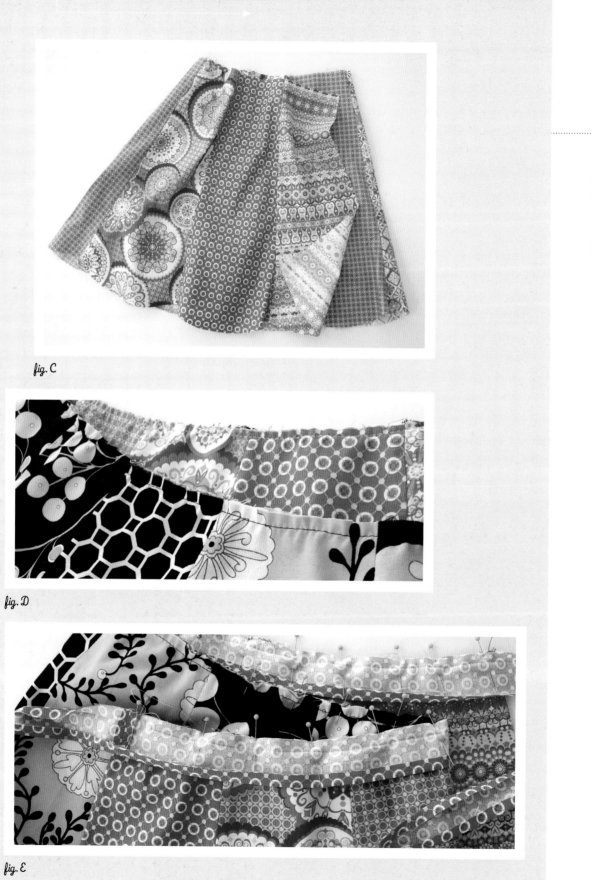

fig. C

fig. D

fig. E

the secondary reversible side

6 With two of the coordinating fabrics and the whole template pattern (taped together if needed), cut three sets of the template pattern and with the third coordinating fabric, cut four sets of the whole template pattern (for a total of 10 sets).

7 Stitch all the segments together, and press the seams open **(fig. C)**.

8 With right sides together, pin the secondary and primary layers together. Stitch one side, turn the corner, stitch the bottom edge, turn the corner, and stitch the other side.

TIP

To turn the corners, place the needle in the down position, pivot the skirt, take one diagonal stitch, and then pivot again and continue stitching.

9 Cut notches on the lower curved edge of the skirt. Turn the skirt right side out, and press.

the waistband

10 Pin together the top edges of the primary and secondary skirt layers, and baste. Slightly gather the baste stitch to cinch the waist **(fig. D)**.

11 From leftover scraps from a primary fabric, use a rotary cutter and cutting mat to create 2-inch-wide (5.1 cm) fabric strips. Join these strips for a final waistband strip that measures 106 inches (269.2 cm) long. (This length depends on the number of skirt segments you use.)

12 Fold under and press each side of the waistband strip $^1/_4$ inch (6 mm). Pin the top edge of the waistband to the top edge of the skirt and stitch **(fig. E)**.

13 Fold the waistband in half to encase the top edge of the skirt, and machine sew in place. Continue sewing the waistband strip to secure the entire length of the ties **(fig. F)**.

14 Fussy cut two circles from one of the coordinating fabrics. Using the fabric circles as templates, cut two circles of batting and backing fabric.

15 Sandwich each circle of batting between a front and backing fabric circle. Pin and stitch through the layers.

16 Stitch a fabric circle to the end of each tie **(fig. G)**.

fig. F

fig. G

Give your dining table some provincial appeal with this custom bistro set. Or make just the napkins for a fancy table setting!

french bistro SET

from your stash

3½ yards (3.2 m) of assorted fabrics (yellows and pinks)

3 yards (2.7 m) pieced backing fabric (approximately 60 x 60 inches [152.4 x 152.4 cm]) or a flat sheet

¼ yard (.2 m) fabric for binding

gather

Basic sewing tool kit (page 7)

Plain white fabric napkins, 18 x 18 inches (45.7 x 45.7 cm)

make

the tablecloth

1 With assorted fabrics, cut 14 strips that are 9 inches (22.9 cm) wide.

2 Cut these strips into 50 squares that measure 9 x 9 inches (22.9 x 22.9 cm). After cutting, you may have a few more squares. Set these extra squares aside to make the matching napkins.

3 Cut these squares on the diagonal to yield 100 half-square triangles (**fig. A**).

4 With right sides together, pair each pink triangle with a yellow triangle, and stitch them together at the diagonal edge.

TIP
If you run out of one color, pair up a pink fabric triangle with another pink fabric triangle or introduce an unexpected fabric from your stash.

fig. A

fig. B

fig. C

fig. D

fig. E

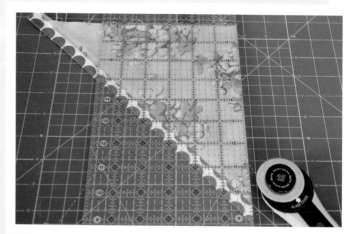

fig. F

❺ Press all seams flat, toward the darker pink fabrics **(fig. B)**. Generally, seam allowances are pressed toward the darker fabrics.

❻ Stack the squares according to the color categories that emerge after the triangles are sewn together.

❼ Using these stacks of squares, sew seven strips of seven squares each. Begin rows 1, 3, 5, and 7 with squares that have pink triangles at the upper left, and begin rows 2, 4, and 6 with squares that have pink triangles at the upper right, as shown in the diagram on page 122. If you run out of squares to fill the pattern exactly, introduce a square constructed with a mix of fabric from your stash.

❽ Press the seams toward the darker pink fabrics.

❾ Line up all the strips in order, from 1 to 7. With right sides together, sew the strips together. Because all seams have been pressed toward the darker pink fabrics, the seams will lock nicely into place.

❿ Measure the quilt top that you have created. Cut or piece a backing that is approximately 1 inch (2.5 cm) longer and wider than the quilt top. Pin the layers together.

⓫ Quilt along the inside edge of each triangle ¹/₄ inch (6 mm) away from the seams. Stitch along the perimeter of the entire quilt **(fig. C)**.

⓬ Measure the perimeter of the quilt. Add 12 inches (30.5 cm) to this measurement to account for turns and overlaps, and cut a 1¹/₂-inch-wide (3.8 cm) binding to the calculated perimeter length. This length should be approximately 6³/₄ yards (6.2 m). With wrong sides together, press the binding in half lengthwise.

⓭ With right sides together, pin and stitch the binding to the edge of the quilt top. Trim excess backing fabric.

⓮ Fold the binding toward the back, turn the edge under by ¹/₄ inch (6 mm), and hand stitch it in place with a slipstitch **(fig. D)**.

the napkins

❶ Using a leftover triangle and binding from the tablecloth project, pin and stitch the binding to the triangle's diagonal edge, right sides together.

❷ Fold the binding to the wrong side of the triangle, and stitch down the binding by stitching in the ditch **(fig. E)**.

❸ Using a quilter's ruler, rotary cutter, and mat, trim excess binding and fabric to create clean triangle edges **(fig. F)**.

❹ Pin the triangle to the napkin at one corner. Use a zigzag stitch to secure the two short sides of the triangle. By keeping the top portion of the triangle open, you will create a pocket into which you can insert flatware.

---

variation!

By switching the colors, you can get a very different look. Go classic in black and white or totally retro in red and aqua.

bento BOX

Everything tastes better in a bento!
Make your own—for dry goods only—
and start packing a lunch you're proud of.

from your stash

¹/₄ yard (.2 m) of fabric A
(aqua flower pattern)

Scraps of fabric B
(stripe pattern)

¹/₃ yard (.3 m) of white binding
fabric

Fabric scraps

¹/₄ yard (.2 m) of fabric D
(diamond pattern)

¹/₄ yard (.2 m) of fabric C
(brown)

gather

Basic sewing tool kit (page 7)

Templates (page 121)

¹/₄ yard (.2 m) of medium-
weight nonwoven interfacing

Spray adhesive

12 inches (30.5 cm) of
hemp yarn

7 x 7-inch (17.8 x 17.8 cm) piece
of muslin

make

cut

1 Using fabrics A and B, cut fabric
pieces as follows:

- For the base of the box: Cut two
  pieces of fabric A that measure
  5¹/₂ x 7¹/₂ inches (14 x 19 cm).
- For the two short sides: Cut two
  pieces of fabric A and two pieces
  of fabric B that each measure
  5 x 2³/₄ inches (12.7 x 7 cm).
- For the two long sides: Cut two
  pieces of fabric A and two pieces
  of fabric B that each measure
  7 x 2³/₄ inches (17.8 x 7 cm).
- For the large center divider:
  Cut two pieces of fabric B
  that measure 5 x 2¹/₂ inches
  (12.7 x 6.4 cm).
- For the small divider: Cut two
  pieces of fabric B that measure
  3¹/₂ x 2¹/₂ inches (8.9 x 6.4 cm).

2 Using the medium-weight nonwoven interfacing, cut the following:

- For the base of the box:
  Cut one piece that measures
  5 x 7 inches (12.7 x 17.8 cm).
- For the two short sides:
  Cut two pieces that measure
  5 x 2¹/₂ inches (12.7 x 6.4 cm).
- For the two long sides:
  Cut two pieces that measure
  7 x 2¹/₂ inches (17.8 x 6.4 cm).
- For the large center divider:
  Cut one piece that measures
  5 x 2¹/₂ inches (12.7 x 6.4 cm).
- For the small divider:
  Cut one piece that measures
  3¹/₂ x 2¹/₂ inches (8.9 x 6.4 cm).

the main box

③ Use spray adhesive to sandwich the pieces of interfacing between the fabric pieces. The interfacing for the base should be centered $^1/_4$ inch (6 mm) from all edges of the fabric base. Align the interfacing for the sides at the top edges and sides of the fabric so that the interfacing will be $^1/_4$ inch (6 mm) away from the bottom edges.

④ With the white fabric, cut and piece a strip of binding that measures $1^1/_8$ inches x 6 yards (2.9 cm x 5.5 m). Fold and press strip lengthwise.

⑤ Use the binding to bind the sides and the top edges of the two large and two small side panels. Then, use the binding to bind all sides of the large and small dividers.

⑥ Machine stitch all four sides to the base of the box **(fig. A)**.

⑦ With a large needle and hemp yarn, tack all sides together at the corners. Insert the inner walls and tack with hemp yarn as well **(fig. B, fig. C)**.

the flap, lid, and ties

⑧ To make the flap, gather random stash fabric strips, piece them together, and true up this patchwork piece to measure 2 x $7^1/_8$ inches (5.1 x 18.1 cm).

⑨ To make the lid, with fabric D, cut one rectangle that measures $7^1/_8$ x $10^1/_8$ inches (5.1 x 25.7 cm) and another rectangle that measures $7^1/_8$ x $8^1/_2$ inches (5.1 x 21.6 cm).

⑩ Sew the patchwork flap to the smaller of the lid pieces.

⑪ To make a pocket for the lid, cut a piece of muslin that measures 6 x 5 inches (15.2 x 12.7 cm). Fold down the top edge 1 inch (2.5 cm), right sides together. Fold this edge up $^1/_4$ inch (6 mm). Stitch the sides of this flap using a $^1/_4$-inch (6 mm) seam allowance. Turn to the right side and press and topstitch across the top of the pocket. Stitch the pocket onto the larger of the lid pieces **(fig. D)**.

⑫ With wrong sides together, machine quilt together the lid pieces, avoiding the area where the pocket has been placed **(fig. E, fig. F)**. Bind the flap and side edges using the leftover binding from step 4.

⑬ To make the ties, cut a strip of white binding fabric that measures 1 x 36 inches (2.5 x 91.4 cm). Fold the strip in half lengthwise and then fold in each lengthwise edge $^1/_4$ inch (6 mm). Stitch together the folded edges.

⑭ Cut a 14-inch (35.6 cm) length from this strip, and tack it, centered, onto the unfinished edge of the lid.

⑮ Cut a 9-inch (22.9 cm) length from the strip, and tack it, centered, onto the bottom edge of the front of the box.

⑯ Stitch the unfinished edge of the lid onto the bottom edge of the back of the box.

fig. A

fig. B

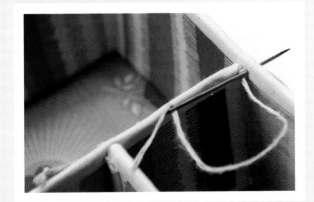

fig. C

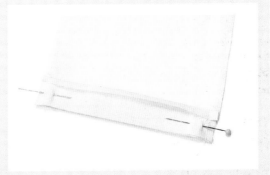

fig. D

fig. E

fig. F

the handles

⑰ Using template A, cut four pieces of fabric C and two pieces of interfacing. Trim ¼-inch (6 mm) strip from the piece of interfacing at the wide edge.

⑱ Using spray adhesive, sandwich each piece of interfacing between two pieces of fabric C. Machine quilt the pieces and bind the outer edges **(fig. F)**.

⑲ Stitch the handles to the outside base of the box, and then bind the base edges **(fig. G)**.

⑳ Close the lid and fasten the ties to secure. Overlap the handles above the box as desired. Use the remaining extra length from the ties to create loops for securing the handles as you carry the box. Hand stitch the loops in place **(fig. H)**.

variation!

Try the same design in oilcloth for added functionality.

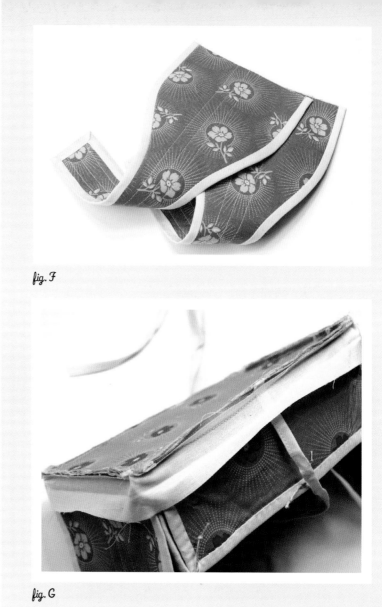

fig. F

fig. G

fig. H

charmed
CANDLE
COZY

Turn your candle into a delightful decoration with this scrap-friendly patchwork cozy.

from your stash

Fabric scraps
(four coordinating colors)

¼ yard (.2 m) of backing fabric

gather

Basic sewing tool kit (page 7)

Embroidery floss or perle cotton

Awl

16 eyelets

Pillar candle in glass jar

¼ yard (.2 m) of batting

1 yard (.9 m) hemp yarn

Charm (optional)

fig. A

fig. B

fig. C

fig. D

fig. E

fig. F

make

❶ With fabric scraps, cut 24 rectangles that measure $2^{1}/_{2}$ x $1^{1}/_{4}$ inches (5.7 x 3.2 cm).

❷ Lay out the rectangles into three columns with eight rectangles in each column **(fig. A)**.

❸ Stitch together the rectangles in each column, and press the seams up on the first and third columns and down on the middle column **(fig. B)**.

❹ Stitch the columns together **(fig. C)**.

❺ Cut the batting $^{1}/_{4}$ inch (6 mm) larger than the quilt top on all sides.

❻ Next, cut the backing fabric to measure $8^{1}/_{4}$ x $7^{1}/_{2}$ inches (21 x 19 cm).

❼ Sandwich together the quilt top, batting, and backing fabric. Quilt these layers by stitching in the ditch at all seams and then around the entire perimeter.

❽ Fold the backing up and over the side edges, and stitch together the backing to the quilt top with a zigzag stitch **(fig. D)**.

❾ With embroidery floss and a sewing needle, hand quilt as desired using a large running stitch **(fig. E)**.

❿ Use an awl to punch eight holes evenly spaced on each side of the cozy. Set an eyelet into each hole.

⓫ Wrap the cozy around a pillar candle in a glass jar, and lace up the eyelets using hemp yarn.

⓬ Adorn the candle with a charm of your choosing, if desired **(fig. F)**.

little sweetheart
DRESS

Pretty in patchwork? Of course! This dress—with cute heart appliqués—is a perfect fit for the little lady in your life.

from your stash

³/₄ yard (.7 m) total of assorted fabrics in coordinating colors

gather

Basic sewing tool kit (page 7)

Template (page 124)

Pencil

²/₃ yard (.6 m) of muslin

42 inches (106.7 cm) of elastic, ¹/₄ inch (6 mm) wide

3 flat buttons

Embroidery floss or perle cotton

3 yards (2.7 m) of ribbon

note: This dress was made to fit girls ages 4 to 5.

make

the skirt & bodice

❶ Using scraps of fabric from your stash in light, medium, and dark colors, cut 42 squares that measure 3³/₄ x 3³/₄ inches (9.5 x 9.5 cm).

❷ Cut these squares on the diagonal to create half-square triangles.

❸ Pair two triangles together, one light and one dark triangle from step 2. With right sides together, sew each pair together along a short side. Press the seam toward the darker fabric **(fig. A)**. Stitch these pieces together to make a square **(fig. B)**.

❹ Repeat step 3 with the remaining triangles.

❺ Using the heart template, trace and cut six hearts from red fabrics.

❻ From lighter fabrics, cut six squares that measure 4¹/₂ x 4¹/₂ inches (11.4 x 11.4 cm). Pin a heart to the center of each of these squares and stitch in place.

❼ Arrange the squares as desired into three rows of nine squares. Stitch the rows in place.

fig. A

fig. B

fig. C

fig. D

fig. E

8 Press the seams on the top and bottom rows in one direction and the seams in the middle row the opposite direction **(fig. C)**. Stitch all three rows together. This patchwork piece is the skirt of the dress.

9 Cut nine rectangles in assorted fabrics that measure 6 x 4^1/$_2$ inches (15.2 x 11.4 cm). Stitch them together along the long edges to create a row. This patchwork piece is the bodice of the dress.

10 Stitch the bodice row to the top of the skirt.

the lining & finishing

11 Using the patchwork dress piece as a template, cut a piece of muslin for the lining.

12 With the dress and lining right sides together, sew the top and bottom edges. At this point, you have a tube with the top of the bodice and bottom of the skirt sewn shut **(fig. D)**.

13 Invert this tube by inserting one of the open sides inward, all the way until the open edges meet. The lining fabric now should be positioned with right sides together, and the dress fabric should be positioned with right sides together.

14 Begin stitching 6 inches (15.2 cm) from the top of the lining fabric layers. Continue sewing so that you stitch past the lining layers and start to sew the dress fabric layers together **(fig. E)**. Stop where the dress fabric meets the lining fabric.

15 Turn the dress right side out by turning the fabric through the opening. Press the dress flat.

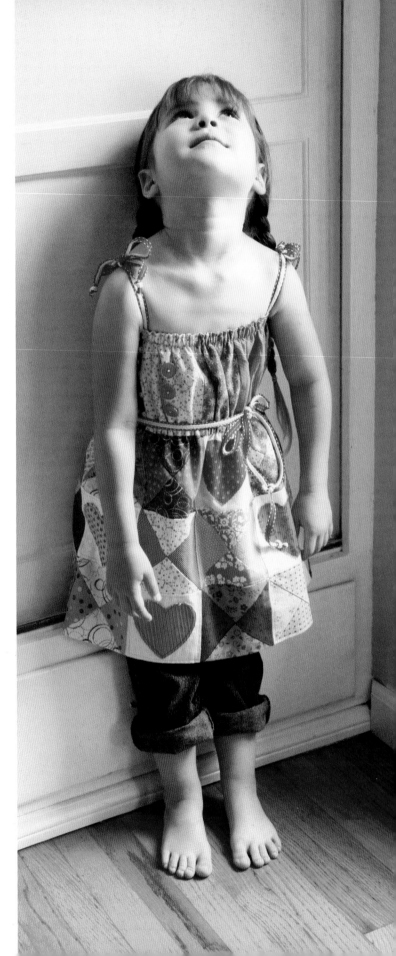

fig. F

fig. G

🔟 Machine quilt the squares $^1/_4$ inch (6 mm) from the seams, skipping every other square, as desired **(fig. F)**.

🔟 Topstitch close to the top edge of the bodice. Then topstitch again, about $^5/_8$ inch (1.6 cm) from the first line of topstitching. The topstitching creates a channel and a small hole through which you will run a length of elastic.

🔟 Repeat step 17 in like fashion for the waist.

🔟 Cut two pieces of elastic that measure 21 inches (53.3 cm) each. Using a safety pin, thread the elastic through the holes and channels at the bodice's top edge and at the waist. Stitch the elastic together, and stitch the hole closed **(fig. G)**.

🔟 Embellish the dress with buttons (sewn on using perle cotton) as desired, and add straps and a belt with ribbon.

This design is totally adjustable!
Make the same design for a doll or for
you by adjusting the number of blocks.
Or, instead of plain lining, use a print
fabric for a reversible dress.

nesting BOWLS

Handy and sweet, these paneled bowls make a great gift. And they're so easy to make! Make a set for a treasured neighbor...and then one for yourself.

from your stash

Fabric scraps (five coordinating colors in small- to medium-sized scraps)

Fabric for bias binding strip, 10 x 10 inches (25.4 x 25.4 cm) (for one bowl)

gather

Basic sewing tool kit (page 7)

Templates (page 120)

$^1/_3$ yard (.3 m) of lightweight nonwoven interfacing

Spray adhesive

fig. A

make

the panels

① Using the side panel template A and four coordinating fabrics, cut two pairs of side panel pieces: Fold fabric, wrong sides together, pin template in place, and cut for eight pairs total.

② Using template B and an additional piece of fabric, cut two bottom pieces.

③ Using template A and the interfacing, cut eight side panel pieces. With template B and the interfacing, cut one bottom piece.

④ Use spray fabric adhesive to sandwich the interfacing panels between each pair of fabric panels and the interfacing bottom between the bottom fabric pieces.

⑤ Align these side panels with the edges of the bottom. Stitch the panels to the bottom piece with a decorative stitch or zigzag stitch **(fig. A)**.

⑥ Pull the two side panels up and stitch together, sewing from the bottom up to the top edge **(fig. B)**. Trim at the top edge where the two panels meet, if needed.

⑦ Repeat with the remaining panels.

finishing

⑧ With the binding fabric, cut and piece a binding strip on the bias that measures $1^{1}/_{4}$ x 35 inches (3.2 x 88.9 cm). Pin the strip to the top edge of the bowl and stitch. Use small stitches and work slowly to maintain the wavy shape of the top edge.

⑨ Turn the binding to the outside. Turn the edge under $^{1}/_{4}$ inch (6 mm) and hand stitch in place **(fig. C)**. Press the bound edges for a clean finish **(fig. D)**.

⑩ Repeat these steps to create bowls in each of the three sizes.

fig. B

fig. C

fig. D

retro APRON

Turn up the heat in the kitchen with this retro apron, made from an upcycled pillowcase. Adorable in every color, make one to match your kitchen décor.

from your stash

Fabric scraps, roughly
4 x 12 inches (10.2 x 30.5 cm)
each (three coordinating colors)

1 piece of fabric for apron
overlay, 15 x 22 inches
(38.1 x 55.9 cm)

$1/4$ yard (.2 m) of coordinating
fabric for the binding
and waistband

$1/3$ yard (.3 m) of main
backing fabric

gather

Basic sewing tool kit (page 7)

Pillowcase (standard size
or larger)

$1/3$ yard (.3 m) of muslin

$1/8$ yard (.1 m) of fusible
interfacing

make

1 Cut the pillowcase to measure 31 x 17 inches (78.7 x 43.2 cm). Reserve extra fabric from the pillowcase to make the apron ties. Turn the outer edges under $1/4$ inch (6 mm) twice and stitch.

the pocket

2 From the three coordinating fabrics, cut nine squares that measure $3^{1}/_{4}$ x $3^{1}/_{4}$ inches (8.3 x 8.3 cm). Organize the squares into a nine-patch block. Stitch together the squares in each row. Then stitch the three rows together **(fig. A)**.

3 Cut a piece of muslin the same size as the nine-patch block.

4 With right sides together, sew three sides of the block and muslin square. Clip the two sewn corners and turn the block right side out. Hand quilt **(fig. B)**.

5 Cut a piece of the fabric for the apron overlay that measures 15 x 22 inches (38.1 x 55.9 cm).

6 Align the unfinished edge of the nine-patch block with a side edge of the overlay. Stitch the finished side and the bottom of the nine patch to the overlay piece to make the pocket. Baste the unfinished edge to the overlay **(fig. C)**.

7 Turn the unfinished edge of the overlay and block under $1/4$ inch (6 mm) twice and topstitch. Sew the bottom and opposite side edges of the overlay in the same way.

8 Center the overlay on the pillowcase fabric. Baste the overlay to the pillowcase $1/2$ inch (1.3 cm) from the top, unfinished overlay edge, and then baste again $1/4$ inch (6 mm) from the same edge.

fig. A

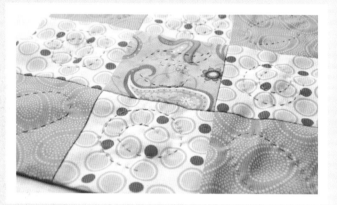

fig. B

fig. C

the waistband

9 To make the waistband, cut two pieces of a coordinating stash fabric and two pieces of fusible interfacing that measure 4$\frac{1}{2}$ x 15 inches (11.4 x 38.1 cm). Fuse the interfacing to the wrong sides of the two fabric pieces.

10 For the ties, cut two pieces of the leftover pillowcase fabric that measure 5 x 30 inches (12.7 x 76.2 cm). Turn three edges of each tie under $\frac{1}{4}$ inch (6 mm) twice, leaving one short edge unfinished. Topstitch.

11 Pull the basting threads on the apron to gather the fabric. With right sides together, pin a waistband piece to the top apron edge, securing the folds. Allow the piece of waistband fabric to extend past both sides of the apron by $\frac{1}{2}$ inch (1.3 cm). Baste in place **(fig. D)**.

12 With right sides together, pin the ties to the ends of the waistband piece that is attached to the apron, aligning the unfinished edges. Add a tuck to the tie, to absorb the extra width and allow $\frac{1}{2}$ inch (1.3 cm) of waistband fabric to extend beyond the tie at the top and bottom edges. Baste in place **(fig. E)**.

13 Place the second piece of waistband fabric face down onto the apron/waistband-in-progress, over the straps that have been sewn to the first waistband piece. Align the top and side edges and then fold up the bottom edge by $\frac{1}{2}$ inch (1.3 cm). Pin and sew up the side, across the top, and then down the other side of the waistband **(fig. F)**.

14 Turn and press all the seam allowances up into the waistband. Blind stitch the back loose edge of the waistband over your previous seam **(fig. G)**. Add decorative hand stitches to the apron as desired.

variation!

Don't have an old pillowcase to spare?
Use a tea towel or a vintage tablecloth,
which are often kitchen themed.

fig. D

fig. E

fig. F

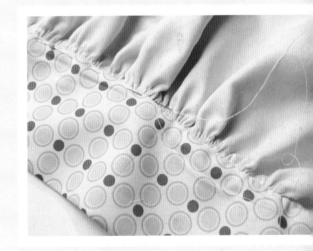

fig. G

sofa arm cozy
& PILLOW

Patchwork makes everything more comfy.
An adjustable arm cozy and pillow are the perfect
additions to your favorite reading nook.

from your stash

$^1/_3$ yard (.3 m) of main fabric

$^1/_4$ yard (.2 m) of coordinating fabric

Fabric scraps (four bold colors and black)

$^1/_4$ yard (.2 m) of black fabric

gather

Basic sewing tool kit (page 7)

$^1/_3$ yard (.3 m) of muslin

1 piece of batting, 12 x 39 inches (30.5 x 99.1 cm)

Perle cotton

60 inches (152.4 cm) of draw-string cording

Polyester fiberfill

make

sofa arm cozy

1 Measure the sofa arm that you wish to cover. With this rough measurement, create a draft of the cozy with a piece of muslin (roughly 14 x 21 inches [35.6 x 53.3 cm]): Fold, gather, and pin the muslin around the sofa arm to get a sense of how the final piece should be cut and sewn.

2 Cut a piece of main fabric from this muslin pattern. Cut the main piece into three pieces as desired and lay strips of coordinating fabric at the cut edges. Stitch the main fabric to the coordinating strips **(fig. A)**.

3 For the backing, piece together large blocks of colorful fabric scraps with black strips.

4 Lay the main pieced block wrong sides together with the colorful block and use the original draft pattern and a rotary cutter or scissors to true up all edges. Use the same pattern to cut a slightly bigger piece of batting.

5 Sandwich the top and bottom pieces with the layer of batting. Baste around the edges.

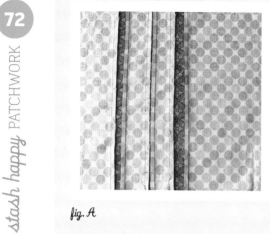

fig. A

fig. B

fig. C

fig. D

variation!

Make a cozy set for your office...
or wherever you surf online
for crafting inspiration!

⑥ With the black fabric, create a binding strip that measures 1¼ inches x 6 yards (3.2 cm x 5.5 m). This strip will create enough binding for the cozy and the pillow.

⑦ Fold the strip in half, pin it to the three straight edges of the pieced top, and stitch. Fold the binding strip over to the back side, and blind stitch to finish.

⑧ Cut a 2¼-inch-wide (6.4 cm) black strip to match the length of the unique curved edge of the cozy. Turn both side ends under ¼ inch (6 mm).

⑨ With right sides together, pin and stitch the strip to the top side of the cozy along the curved edge.

⑩ Fold over and hand stitch the strip along the other side of the curve **(fig. B)**. Because this strip is wider than traditional binding, there will be enough room for a cord to be threaded through this space to cinch the cozy close to the sofa's arm.

⑪ With a needle and perle cotton, add hand quilting to both sides of the cozy, being careful to only quilt through the top fabric and batting of either side **(fig. C)**.

⑫ Pull the drawstring cording through the curved black binding, cinch, and tie **(fig. D)**.

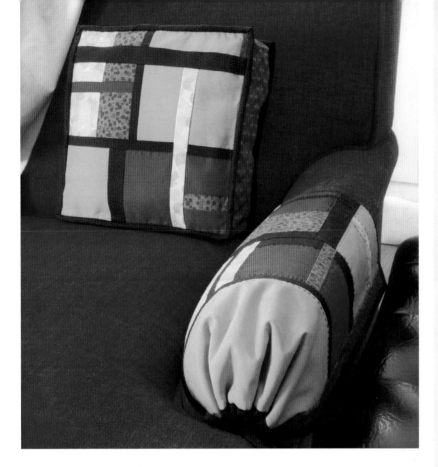

the pillow

 Make a square patchwork block for the pillow by cutting an 11-inch (27.9 cm) square from the main fabric, cutting it in three places, and inserting coordinating strips **(fig. E)**. For the back, create a block using the colorful stash fabrics and black strips **(fig. F)**.

 True up both blocks to measure 10 $^1/_2$ x 10 $^1/_2$ inches (26.7 x 26.7 cm). Cut two pieces of batting and two pieces of muslin to the same dimensions. Layer each patchwork block with the batting in the middle and muslin on the back and hand quilt.

 From the coordinating fabric, cut four side panels that measure 3$^1/_2$ x 10$^1/_2$ inches (8.9 x 26.7 cm).

④ Stitch the short ends of the panel pieces together, leaving $^1/_4$ inch (6 mm) unstitched at the start and

finish of each stitch line **(fig. G)**. Press the seams open.

⑤ With wrong sides together, pin the stitched panels to the quilted pillow square. There will be a natural opening at each corner, created by the $^1/_4$-inch (6 mm) opening at the start and finish of each strip, allowing for ease of turn and sewing.

⑥ Sew the front and back sides of the pillow to the side panels, leaving a small section unstitched. Stuff the pillow with polyester fiberfill, and stitch the opening closed.

⑦ Use the leftover binding from the arm cozy to bind the edges of the pillow **(fig. H)**.

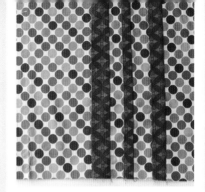

fig. E

fig. F

fig. G

fig. H

For those extra cold days, here's a special hooded scarf made from comfy flannel. It's completely reversible and will keep you covered from the neck up.

scrappy SCOODIE

from your stash

1/2 yard (.5 m) of brown fabric scraps

1/2 yard (.5 m) of blue fabric scraps

2 pieces of brown fabric (for hood), 12 x 24 inches (30.5 x 61 cm)

2 pieces of blue fabric (for hood), 12 x 24 inches (30.5 x 61 cm)

Stash fabric scraps (for star block)

gather

Basic sewing tool kit (page 7)

Template (page 120)

Pencil

Spray adhesive

60 inches (152.4 cm) of draw-string cording

Perle cotton

make

the scarf & hood

❶ To create the scarf sections, piece together assorted brown fabrics to make a piece of fabric that measures 7 x 75 inches (17.8 x 190.5 cm). Repeat in like fashion with assorted blue fabrics. Or, you may want to use a single piece of fabric cut to this size.

❷ Using template A, cut two pieces from the brown and from the blue fabrics. Mark notches at the face opening.

❸ With right sides together, stitch the brown pieces together along the curved edges, using a 1/2-inch (1.3 cm) seam allowance. Repeat in like fashion to make the blue hood **(fig. A)**.

❹ Turn the brown hood right side out. Place the brown hood inside the blue hood with right sides together, and pin. Double pin at the notches; you will not sew between the double pins. Using a 1/2-inch (1.3 cm) seam allowance, stitch both layers of the hood together at the front opening. Turn the hood right side out.

❺ Press the seam open, and topstitch on both sides of the seam, catching the seam allowance to reveal the openings for the cording **(fig. B)**.

❻ Tuck one hood into the other, and stitch 3/4 inch (1.9 cm) from the front opening edge. This will create a channel for the cording **(fig. C)**.

fig. A

fig. B

fig. C

the star block

7 To make first star block, with stash fabric, cut 13 squares that each measure $2^1/_4$ x $2^1/_4$ inches (5.7 x 5.7 cm). Use dark colored fabric for nine of the squares and bright colored fabric for four of the squares.

8 With right sides together, pair a bright and a dark square. Mark a diagonal line from corner to corner.

9 Stitch just alongside the marked line. Trim off the excess to a $1/_4$-inch (6 mm) seam allowance. Before sewing, you may want to decide which corners you will trim. Press the seam toward the dark fabric.

10 Repeat steps 8 and 9 in like fashion to make four pieced squares.

11 Arrange the pieced and plain squares to create a star pattern as shown **(fig. D)**.

12 Stitch together the squares to create three rows. Then, stitch the rows together to form a completed block **(fig. E)**.

13 Repeat steps 7 through 12 for the second star block.

finishing

14 With right sides together, align the center back of the hood with the center back of one of the scarf sections (from step 1). Pin and sew using a $1/_2$-inch (1.3 cm) seam allowance **(fig. F)**.

15 Lay the second scarf section down onto the first, right sides together. Roll the hood up between the scarf layers. Pin and sew along all sides, leaving a 7-inch (17.8 cm) opening on the long straight side of the scarf where the hood is stitched to the first scarf section **(fig. G)**.

16 Clip the corners of the scarf and turn it right side out. Fold under the fabric at the opening, and topstitch to close.

17 With spray adhesive, position the star block onto the hood. Zigzag stitch the block to secure it in place. Machine quilt as desired. Repeat in like fashion to attach the remaining star block to the other side of the hood **(fig. H)**.

18 Thread the drawstring cording through the hood.

fig. D

fig. E

fig. F

fig. G

fig. H

variation!

Make your scoodie out of clothing instead. A soft, worn-in flannel shirt, a collection of old cotton tees, or leftover fleece would all be cozy and warm.

log cabin BUCKET

Four log cabin blocks create the pockets on this handy bucket. It makes a great toy tote and works extra hard on road trips.

from your stash

Fabric scraps and strips

¹/₄ yard (.2 m) of tan burlap

¹/₂ yard (.5 m) of dark brown burlap

¹/₂ yard (.5 m) of tan canvas

¹/₃ yard (.3 m) of dark brown canvas

gather

Basic sewing tool kit (page 7)

Templates (page 121)

Sheet of cardstock

¹/₄ yard (.2 m) of muslin

1 yard (1 m) of twill tape binding, 1¹/₄ inch (3.2 cm) wide

Nonwoven interfacing

30 inches (76.2 cm) of strapping

1 overall buckle

2 overall buttons

make

the blocks & lining

❶ With right sides together, create the block's center and first log by placing a small 1¹/₂ x 2-inch (3.8 x 5.1 cm) fabric rectangle onto a slightly longer fabric strip. Sew the edges together along one long edge. Then, trim the excess fabric from the strip **(fig. A)**.

❷ Open the sewn pieces with wrong sides facing you. Rotate the block so that the strip you just added is at the top. Press the seam toward the center.

❸ With the right sides together, place the next fabric strip beneath the center, right edges aligned. Stitch the right edges together, trim the excess fabric, and press the seam toward the center **(fig. B)**.

❹ Repeat steps 2 and 3, sewing, trimming, and pressing logs around the center and tiers of logs until the block is slightly larger than 8 x 8 inches (20.3 x 20.3 cm). As you continue working, the strips will need to get longer as the block gets larger. Vary the width of the strips to make the block uniquely wonky.

❺ Cut a template from card-stock that measures 8 x 8 inches (20.3 x 20.3 cm). Place the template on top of the pieced block, and angle the template slightly

fig. A

fig. B

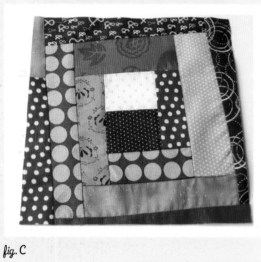

fig. C

fig. D

fig. E

for a wonkier log cabin block. Use a quilter's ruler, cutting mat, and rotary cutter to trim the edges of the pieced block **(fig. C)**.

6 Using this technique, repeat steps 1 to 5 to create a total of four blocks.

7 Using template A, cut four wedge-shaped pieces from the tan burlap. With right sides together, pin the shapes between the blocks and stitch them together. The added pieces will cause the final patchwork piece to slightly arc **(fig. D)**.

8 Lay this arc-shaped patchwork piece onto the muslin and cut a muslin lining. Stitch the side seams of the muslin lining together. This will be the center back.

9 With right sides together, connect the ends of the large arc-shaped patch-work piece by stitching the last wedge to the first wonky square block.

10 Place the muslin lining into the patchwork piece, wrong sides together. Pin and baste.

11 Cut a strip of binding from the tan burlap that measures $1^3/_8$ x $32^1/_2$ inches (3.5 x 82.6 cm).

12 Use the burlap binding to encase the top edges of the patchwork and lining pieces and sew together with a wide zigzag stitch.

13 Cut four 1-inch (2.5 cm) squares of burlap and zigzag stitch one square to the center of each block. Add machine quilting around some of the wonky logs, as desired **(fig. E)**.

fig. F

fig. G

fig. H

the bucket

⓮ Cut a piece of dark brown burlap and a piece of tan canvas that each measure 14 x 32 inches (35.6 x 81.3 cm).

⓯ With right sides together, stitch the top edge of the burlap and canvas together. Unfold the layers flat, and then fold the short sides together, with right sides facing. Stitch along the short sides, starting with the burlap, then into the canvas **(fig. F)**. Turn right side out and move the seam to the center back. This will be the body of the bucket. Zigzag stitch around the top edge.

⓰ Stitch the bottom edges of the patchwork and lining layers to the bottom edge of the bucket **(fig. G)**.

⓱ Pin the top portion of the patched piece to the bucket to create pockets. Place pins strategically so that each pocket bows out consistently. Use a zigzag stitch to create the pockets, sewing from the bottom of the bucket to the top. Turn the bucket inside out.

⓲ Use template B to cut two circles, one from dark brown canvas and one from tan canvas. Stack the circles wrong sides together and pin them to the bottom of the bucket making sure the canvas will be on the inside. Stitch around the circles to secure them to the bucket **(fig. H)**.

⓳ With 1¼-inch-wide (3.2 cm) twill tape binding, encase the bottom seam with a zigzag stitch.

the strap

⓴ Cut a strip of fabric and nonwoven interfacing that each measure 1½ x 30 inches (3.8 x 76.2 cm).

㉑ Lay the fabric strip on the nonwoven interfacing and fold under both sides of these layers by ¼ inch (6 mm). Stitch the layers onto the 1½-inch (3.8 cm) strapping.

㉒ Stitch one end of the strap down and into one of the pockets **(fig. I)**. Loop the opposite end of the strap into an overall buckle. Fold the exposed strap end under twice and stitch it in place by machine or hand.

㉓ Attach two overall buttons, one directly opposite the strap and the other 4 inches (10.2 cm) away from the first; the second button is used when the bucket is hanging.

fig. I

doggone
DOG COLLAR

Take your pooch for a stroll in style! This oh-so-chic collar
is easy to adjust for any size dog.

from your stash

¹/₈ yard (.1 m) of fabric
(three coordinating colors)

gather

Basic sewing tool kit (page 7)

Safety pin

Embroidery floss

Scrap of batting

Dog collar

1 flat button

make

the collar

➊ From two coordinating fabrics, cut one strip that measures 1¹/₄ x 10 inches (3.2 x 25.4 cm).

➋ With a third coordinating fabric, cut one strip that measure 2 x 10 inches (5.1 x 25.4 cm).

➌ Stitch the three strips together along the long edges, with the widest strip in the middle.

➍ Using a rotary cutter, cut the sewn strip into pieces that measure 2³/₄ x 2³/₄ inches (7 x 7 cm) **(fig. A)**. Depending on the size of the dog collar, you may need to make more pieces strips to work from.

➎ Stitch together the pieces. For this collar, three pieces were sewn together.

➏ Topstitch along the seam lines. Fold under ¹/₄ inch (6 mm) on both ends and stitch down.

➐ With right sides together, fold the collar piece lengthwise, and stitch together the long edges using a ¹/₄-inch (6 mm) seam allowance **(fig. B)**.

➑ Attach a safety pin to one end and pull it through the collar piece to turn the collar right side out.

➒ Using embroidery floss and a sewing needle, sew a running stitch along the long edges **(fig. C)**.

➓ Fussy cut two circles (or other motifs) from one of the fabrics. Using the cut circle as a template, cut a piece of batting.

⑪ Sandwich the piece of batting between the two circles, and use embroidery floss and a sewing needle to secure them together with a blanket stitch.

⑫ Attach the sewn circle onto the patchwork collar.

⑬ Insert the dog collar into the patchwork collar, and attach a button to finish.

variation!

Use the same basic steps for the collar to make a whole patchwork leash. You'll have plenty of time to show it off on those long neighborhood walks.

fig. A

fig. B

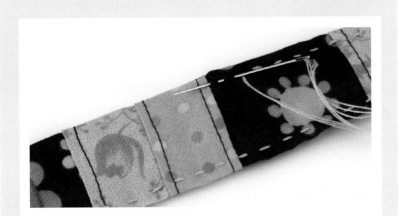

fig. C

online!

Download instructions for a matching bag—perfect for toting plastic bags, treats, or leash storage— at www.larkcrafts.com/bonus.

dresden plate RUG

A classic block gets a modern twist with this spot-on patchwork rug. You might love it too much to put on the floor, in which case it makes a lovely wall hanging.

from your stash

Fabric scraps (five coordinating colors)

⅛ yard (.1 m) of fabric (for binding)

gather

Basic sewing tool kit (page 7)

Templates (page 125)

½ yard (.5 m) of batting

Spray adhesive

Jute rug, 24 x 36 inches (61 x 91.4 cm)

Heavy cotton thread

White acrylic paint

Small paintbrush

make

the dresden plate blocks

① Using templates A, B, and C and coordinating fabrics, cut 13 petal pieces from each template. These pieces will create one large, one medium, and one small Dresden plate block.

② Fold one petal in half, right sides together, and stitch across the top. Clip the folded corner and press the seams open. Then turn the petal right side out and press **(fig. A)**. When you press, align the top point with the center of the bottom edge of the petal. Consistency in this alignment will ensure that all petals match up when sewing them together to complete the Dresden plate block.

③ Repeat step 2 for all the petal pieces.

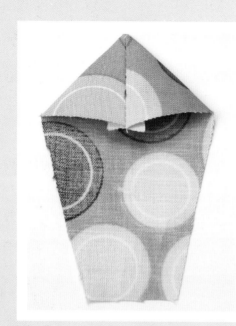

fig. A

fig. B

fig. C

fig. D

fig. E

④ With right sides together, stitch two prepared petals along one side. Press open the seam. Repeat to complete each Dresden plate block **(fig. B)**.

⑤ Cut a square of batting slightly larger than each block. Apply fabric spray adhesive to the back side of each pieced block and place them onto the corresponding batting piece. Pin the layers together.

⑥ Trim away excess batting around each Dresden plate block. Once cut, trim again around the petal points of the batting so it is slightly smaller than the pieced blocks **(fig. C)**.

⑦ With coordinating fabric, cut a binding strip on the bias that measures 1^1/$_4$ x 35 inches (3.2 x 88.9 cm). Fold the strip in half. Pin the strip to the patchwork layer of each block along the round center edge. Stitch the binding **(fig. D)**.

⑧ Cut out the excess batting from the center of the Dresden plate block. Fold the binding strip over the edge of the circle and to the back. Stitch in the ditch—between the binding and the petals—to secure.

⑨ Apply fabric spray adhesive to the quilt block and place it onto the rug. Reinforce the placement with pins, and, using heavy cotton thread, hand sew the block in place using a slipstitch. Repeat with the remaining Dresden plate blocks.

finishing

⑩ If desired, paint circles in the middle of the blocks with white acrylic paint.

⑪ The finished measurement for my rug is 24 x 36 inches (61 x 91.4 cm). Depending on the size of your finished rug, complete the project by adding a matching binding strip to the edges of the rug **(fig. E)**.

clothespin CADDY

Pretty up your laundry day!
Stitch the perfect holder for
all kinds of clips and pins.

from your stash

Fabric scraps (seven coordinating colors) (enough for one
10-inch [25.4 cm] square and
twelve 3-inch [7.6 cm] squares)

$2/3$ yard (.6 m) of main fabric

gather

Basic sewing tool kit (page 7)

Templates (page 120)

Spray adhesive

$1/4$ yard (.2 m) of muslin

Clothing hanger

Ribbon

note: These instructions have
been created to fit a vintage
wooden hanger with the
ends sawn off. Compare your
hanger to the template and
adjust the size of your bag
as needed.

make

the main pocket

1 Using template A and the main
fabric, cut three pieces, making sure
to mark the notches at the top. Cut a
coordinating fabric to 10 x 10 inches
(25.4 x 25.4 cm).

2 Center and stitch the 10-inch
(25.4 cm) square piece of fabric to
the wrong side of an A piece.

3 Using template A, mark and cut
out large holes, centered, from the two
remaining A pieces. With right sides
together, sew the A pieces together
along the cut circle edges. Make small
snips toward the stitch line of the
sewn circle edges **(fig. A)**.

4 Turn right side out. Press the circle
and topstitch $1/4$ inch (6 mm) from the
stitched edge.

the front pockets

5 Cut 12 squares in coordinating
fabrics that measure $2^3/4$ x $2^3/4$ inches
(7 x 7 cm). Using template B and coordinating fabrics, cut three circles.

6 With right sides together, stitch the
squares together in pairs. Stitch two
pairs together to make a square block.
Repeat with the remaining pairs to
make three blocks.

fig. A

fig. B

fig. C

fig. D

fig. E

7 Apply spray adhesive to the wrong sides of the fabric circles from step 5. Place a circle onto the center of each pieced block. Zigzag stitch around each circle to secure **(fig. B)**.

8 Cut two muslin strips that measure 1 x 5 inches (2.5 x 12.7 cm). Line up the blocks in a horizontal row, placing a muslin strip between the blocks. Stitch the muslin strips to the blocks.

9 Cut a strip from muslin that measures $1^1/_2$ x 65 inches (3.8 x 165.1 cm). Press the strip in half lengthwise to create binding.

10 Stitch the binding strip along the top edge of the patchwork piece. Flip over the binding and stitch in the ditch from the right side **(fig. C)**.

11 Pin and stitch down the sides and across the bottom of the patchwork piece to the main pocket piece A with the hole cut in the middle.

12 Stitch in the ditch on both sides of the muslin strips to make the three pockets.

13 With right sides together, place this patchwork piece onto the remaining A piece. Stitch together the two pieces across the top edges, leaving an opening at the notches **(fig. D)**. Turn right side out and press the seam open.

14 Topstitch on both sides of the seam, catching the seam allowance. This opening at the top of the bag creates a hole for the hanger hook to extend through the bag.

15 While the bag is right side out, stitch closed the side and bottom edges. Using the leftover binding from step 9, bind these edges by first sewing the binding to the front edges, then folding over the strip to the back side of the bag and stitching the binding in place with a blind stitch **(fig. E)**.

16 Insert the hanger and tie a scrap of fabric (or decorative ribbon) around the opening, as desired.

sew on the go KIT

With the help of your stash, you'll soon be ready to bring the (quilt) show on the road.

from your stash

Fabric scraps (three coordinating colors)

1¼ x 16 inches (3.2 x 40.6 cm) of fabric for binding

gather

Basic sewing tool kit (page 7)

Templates (page 125)

Muslin scraps

Lightweight and heavyweight nonwoven interfacing scraps

Spray adhesive

Polyester fiberfill

17 inches (43.2 cm) of ribbon

1 flat button

1 felt flower or scrap of felt

make

1 With three coordinating fabrics, cut five 9-inch-long (22.9 cm) strips in three different widths, from 1 to 3 inches (2.5 to 7.6 cm) wide. Arrange the strips as desired and stitch them together to make a pieced block.

2 Using template A, cut two pieces from the pieced block. Tilt or angle the template before cutting. Then, use template A to cut one piece from a piece of coordinating fabric and three pieces from muslin **(fig. A)**.

3 Using the templates, cut the following:
- Template B: Cut three pieces of lightweight nonwoven interfacing.
- Template C: Cut one piece from a coordinating fabric.
- Template D: Cut two pieces from a coordinating fabric.
- Template E: Cut one piece from a coordinating fabric.
- Template F: Cut three pieces from muslin.
- Template G: Cut one piece of heavyweight nonwoven interfacing.

fig. A

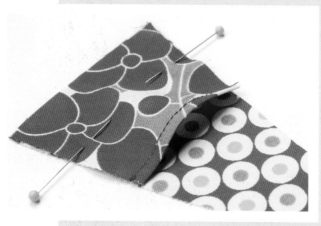

fig. B

the side panels

❹ Fold under the top edge of the fabric piece cut from template C and stitch. Pin and baste the C piece to the A piece cut from the coordinating fabric. The top edge of the C piece will naturally bow out **(fig. B)**.

❺ Fold under and stitch the top edges of the D pieces. Then, fold under the sides and bottom edge $^1/_4$ inch (6 mm). Stitch the D pieces onto two muslin A pieces, $^3/_4$ inch (1.9 cm) from the bottom edges **(fig. C)**.

❻ Apply spray adhesive to the pieces of lightweight interfacing, and place them onto the wrong sides of the fabric A pieces. Quilt along the pieced seams **(fig. D)**.

❼ With right sides together, stitch a fabric A piece to a muslin A piece, leaving the bottom edge open. Clip the corners and add a small horizontal snip at both sides of the "neck." Repeat for the other two sides.

❽ Turn the side panels right side out and press. Then turn the bottom edges of the panels under by $^1/_4$ inch (6 mm) and blind stitch closed.

fig. C

fig. D

the pincushion

9 With wrong sides together, sew together each short side of the three muslin F pieces to form a pyramid shape **(fig. E)**.

10 Apply spray adhesive to the heavyweight interfacing, and place it onto the wrong side of piece E. Hand stitch the fabric pyramid onto this prepared piece. Before stitching closed the final edge, stuff the pincushion with fiberfill, then stitch closed.

11 Cut a strip of binding that measures $1^{1}/_{4}$ x 16 inches (3.2 x 40.6 cm). Machine stitch the strip around the inside edge of the pincushion base **(fig. F)**. Fold the binding over the pincushion edges, and blind stitch to finish.

12 Stitch the three side panels to the pincushion base **(fig. G)**.

finishing

13 With a small flat button, attach a felt flower on top of the pincushion.

14 Hand-tack the ribbon to the outside of one of the panels at the neck.

15 Fill the finished pincushion and panel pockets with sewing notions. Tie the ribbon around the panels to close.

fig. E

fig. F

fig. G

cupcake FLAGS

This small set is the ideal companion for a baked gift—and they whip up faster than the frosting.

from your stash

Fabric scraps
(five coordinating colors)

gather

Basic sewing tool kit (page 7)

Templates (page 121)

Scrap of batting

Acrylic paint

Embroidery floss

1 wooden skewer

make

the heart

❶ With four coordinating fabrics, cut four squares that measure 2 x 2 inches (5.1 x 5.1 cm) **(fig. A)**.

❷ Stitch two squares together and press the seam to the right. Stitch the two remaining squares together and press the seam to the left. Stitch together these two pieces, and press the final seam up toward the top two blocks **(fig. B)**.

❸ Cut a piece of backing fabric and batting slightly larger than the pieced top.

❹ Pin a template to the pieced top, and cut around the template, allowing an extra ¹/₄ inch (6 mm) all around the template **(fig. C)**.

fig. A

fig. B

fig. C

fig. D

fig. E

5 Machine quilt, creating a center channel that allows the skewer to be inserted **(fig. D)**.

6 With acrylic paint, paint a wooden skewer in a color that coordinates with the quilted top.

7 Add hand stitches (using embroidery floss) to the quilted top as desired, and insert the dry, painted skewer into the shape **(fig. E)**.

variations!

Make the other template designs (the butterfly, banner, and wings) using similar piecing and quilting techniques. Be sure to create channels in all the designs that allow the skewers to be inserted.

vested INTEREST

Sewing garments for little boys is every bit as fun as it is for little girls. This vest project makes the most of one main fabric and several scraps in blue.

from your stash

Blue fabric scraps

¹/₂ yard (.5 m) of main fabric

¹/₂ yard (.5 m) of front lining fabric

¹/₂ yard (.5 m) of backing fabric

gather

Basic sewing tool kit (page 7)

Templates (page 126)

¹/₄ yard (.2 m) of interfacing

3 buttons, ⁵/₈ inch (1.6 cm) diameter

Embroidery floss

Fabric marker

make

the patchwork front

1 Using template F and blue stash fabric scraps, cut eight diamonds.

2 Using template G and the main fabric, cut 20 triangles.

3 Position the diamonds and triangles as shown, and sew the top left triangle to the first blue diamond. Then, sew on the triangle to the bottom right of that diamond. Repeat in like fashion with the remaining three diamonds **(fig. A)**.

fig. A

❹ Sew the four diamond segments together, and press the seams toward each diamond shape. Sew a triangle to the bottom left and top right of the entire patchwork piece.

❺ Repeat steps 3 and 4 to create another patchwork panel with the remaining four diamonds. Be sure that the blue fabric used for the center front diamonds matches so the diamonds will overlap nicely when the vest is buttoned.

❻ Lay template C on top of the two patchwork pieces which are laying right sides together, and true up the side and front seams.

❼ Using template A and the main fabric, cut two pieces: Fold the fabric right sides together, and cut the folded fabric to yield two pieces—one for the left and one for the right side of the vest. Cut two pieces in like fashion using template B and the main fabric.

❽ Pin and sew the patchwork pieces with the A and B pieces for both the left and right sides of the vest using a ¹⁄₄-inch (6 mm) seam allowance **(fig. B)**.

fig. B

the lining & assembly

9 Using these sewn vest fronts as templates, lay each onto the front lining fabric, wrong sides together, and cut two pieces of lining fabric.

10 Using template D and the back fabric, cut two pieces. The fabric used for the back's exterior and lining is the same fabric. Make cuts at all notches and markings at all dots.

11 Using template E and the interfacing, cut two pieces on fabric that has been folded. Fuse the interfacing to the wrong side of the front edge of the front lining fabric.

12 With the back fabric, cut two pieces that measure 2 x 12 inches (5.1 x 30.5 cm) for the straps. (For size medium, cut 13-inch-long [33 cm] straps; for large, cut 14-inch-long [35.6 cm] straps.)

13 Prepare a strap by folding one end under by $^1/_4$ inch (6 mm). Fold the strap in half lengthwise and turn under the long edges $^1/_4$ inch (6 mm). Topstitch the folded edges together. Repeat in like fashion for the second strap.

14 At the notches, baste the straps to the side seams of the back piece. Stitch the strap securely at the dots **(fig. C)**.

15 Press the back lining shoulder seams toward the wrong side $^1/_2$ inch (1.3 cm). With right sides together, pin the back lining to the front lining at the side seams and sew. Press the seams open.

16 With right sides together, pin the back (with the straps) to the two front patchwork pieces and sew the side seams together using a $^1/_2$-inch (1.3 cm) seam allowance. Press the seams open.

17 You now have two vests. With right sides together pin the vests together around the perimeter edges, but do not pin the shoulder seams. Leave those areas open **(fig. D)**.

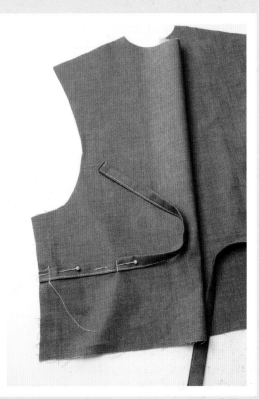

fig. C

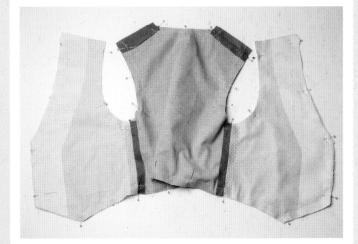

fig. D

fig. E

fig. F

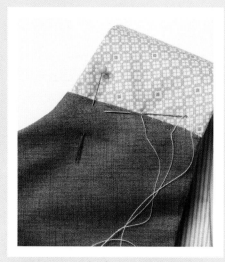

fig. G

fig. H

18 Sew around the pinned areas using a $^1/_2$-inch (1.3 cm) seam allowance. Trim the seam allowance down to $^1/_4$ inch (6 mm). Clip into every curve, and trim every corner.

19 Turn the entire vest right side out through one of the back shoulder openings. Press the vest thoroughly, making sure that all pointed edges are sharp **(fig. E)**.

20 With right sides together, pin the shoulder seams together. Do not catch the back lining's pressed seam allowance **(fig. F)**. Stitch closed using a $^1/_2$-inch (1.3 cm) seam allowance. Turn all seam allowances toward the back, and hand stitch the lining shoulder seam in place **(fig. G)**.

finishing

21 Topstitch close to the edge around the perimeter of the vest and armhole **(fig. H)**. Hand quilt around the diamond shapes with embroidery floss.

22 Add three buttons and buttonholes. Sew three buttonholes horizontally on the left side for boys and on the right for girls.

wonky cottage LAP QUILT

Cozy up on the porch under this wonderfully wonky lap quilt.

Off-kilter house blocks and stitched details add to the charm.

from your stash

Fabric scraps, ten to fifteen
6 x 6-inch (15.2 x 15.2 cm) squares
in coordinating colors

1¼ yards (1.1 m) of white and
off-white fabrics

⅓ yard (.3 m) of coordinating
fabric for binding

¼ yard (.2 m) of coordinating
fabric for straps

1⅜ yards (1.3 m) of backing
fabric and muslin

gather

Basic sewing tool kit (page 7)

Templates (page 123)

Embroidery floss

1⅜ yards (1.3 m) of batting

Embroidery thread

*note: finished measurement is
40 x 55 inches (101.6 x 139.7 cm).*

make

the wonky house blocks

① Gather the stash fabrics in assorted
colors and use roof templates A, B,
and C to cut six A roofs, six B roofs,
and six C roofs. From the white fabrics, cut 18 strips that measure
4½ x 18 inches (11.4 x 45.7 cm).
Each house block uses one strip.

② From one of the white strips, cut a
portion that measures 10¼ inches
(26 cm) in length. Lay roof A onto the
10¼-inch (26 cm) strip of white fabric, centering the bottom edge of the
roof on the strip.

③ Using a quilter's ruler, cutting mat,
and rotary cutter, cut the white fabric
along the roofline. Remove the white
fabric underneath the patterned fabric
roof and stitch the patterned roof
piece to the white background pieces
along the roofline **(fig. A)**.

④ Repeat steps 2 to 3 for the remaining A, B, and C houses.

⑤ For each house block A, cut one
piece of coordinating fabric that measures 4½ x 5 inches (11.4 x 12.7 cm).
From the remainder of a white fabric
strip, cut two pieces that measure
4½ x 2¼ inches (11.4 x 5.7 cm).
Sew together the fabric pieces to complete the house portion of each block
(fig. B).

fig. A

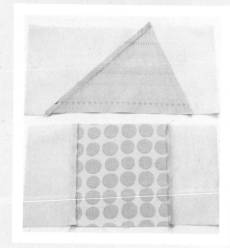

fig. B

fig. C

⑥ Stitch together the pieced top and bottom portions of each block. You will notice a slight bit of excess fabric on the top portions of the blocks. This extra fabric allows you to exaggerate the "wonkiness" of the house block, if desired, by nudging the roof a bit more to one side. After piecing, flip over the entire wonky house block, press the block, and use a rotary cutter to trim off excess fabric so that it measures 8$^1/_2$ x 8$^1/_2$ inches (21.6 x 21.6 cm) **(fig. C)**.

⑦ Using the same techniques as for wonky house block A, use the following measurements to create wonky house blocks B and C:

• For each block B: Cut a piece of coordinating fabric that measures 4$^1/_2$ x 4 inches (11.4 x 10.2 cm). From the remainder of a white fabric strip, cut two pieces that measure 4$^1/_2$ x 2$^3/_4$ inches (11.4 x 7 cm).

• For each block C: Cut a piece of coordinating fabric that measures 4$^1/_2$ x 4$^1/_2$ inches (11.4 x 11.4 cm). From the remainder of a white fabric strip, cut two pieces that measure 4$^1/_2$ x 2$^1/_2$ inches (11.4 x 6.4 cm).

⑧ From your fabric stash, cut small rectangles and trapezoids to make doors and windows. There are no templates for these pieces. Dare to exaggerate proportions to achieve a playful look. Pin and zigzag stitch in place **(fig. D)**.

finishing

⑨ From assorted white fabrics, cut 17 blocks that measure 8$^1/_2$ x 8$^1/_2$ inches (21.6 x 21.6 cm). Line up the house blocks, alternating with the white blocks, to create a total of seven rows. Stitch together the blocks in each row. Press the seams toward the solid white blocks. Then stitch the rows together.

⑩ If needed, piece together coordinating fabrics to create a backing that measures 43 x 57 inches (109.2 x 144.8 cm). Layer the quilt top with the batting and backing, and pin the layers together.

⑪ Stitch in the ditch around all the blocks. Then free-motion quilt in the large white squares, and topstitch $^1/_4$ inch (6 mm) from the seams around the roofs and houses. Use embroidery floss to add hand quilting around the windows and doors of some of the houses.

⑫ Cut fabric for binding that is 2$^1/_4$ inches (5.7 cm) wide and 6 yards (5.5 m) long. Press the fabric in half lengthwise. Pin and stitch the binding to the outside edge of the quilt top **(fig. E)**. Trim any excess from the fabric layers.

⑬ Turn the binding over the edge and blind stitch the binding in place.

fig. D

fig. E

the shoulder strap

14 From a coordinating fabric, cut two strips that measure 4 x 32 inches (10.2 x 81.3 cm) and one strip that measures 2 x 7 inches (5.1 x 17.8 cm).

15 Fold the larger strips in half lengthwise with right sides together, and stitch, using a $^1/_4$-inch (6 mm) seam allowance, pivoting at the corner on one end of each strip. Clip the corners diagonally and turn the strips right side out.

16 Fold the quilt in half lengthwise and roll it up. Mark 6 inches (15.2 cm) from the outer bound edge and the folded edge just above the binding on the quilt. Sew a long strip at each mark **(fig. F)**.

17 Press the smaller strip in half lengthwise and then press in both unfinished edges $^1/_4$ inch (6 mm). Stitch the strip closed along the folded edge. Cut the strip into two pieces measuring $3^1/_2$ inches (8.9 cm).

18 While the quilt is rolled up, mark placement for the smaller strips, which will serve as loops. Fold the ends of the smaller strips under $^1/_4$ inch (6 mm). Place them on the quilt, lining them up with the straps, about 7 inches (17.8 cm) from the bound and folded edges of the quilt. Allow the strips to bow just a little, then stitch in place to make loops.

19 Thread the straps through the loops and tie the straps in a bow as desired to create a shoulder strap.

variation!

Make the quilt to match your neighborhood. Surrounded by greenery? Nestle your houses among patchwork trees. Need something more urban? Try little wonky apartment buildings.

 fig. F

hobo BAG

This patchwork bag is for the girl who has everything (and must take it around town with her).

from your stash

¹/₂ yard (.5 m) of main fabric

Fabric stash ranging from ¹/₁₆ to ¹/₄ yard (5 cm to .2 m) (five coordinating colors)

gather

Basic sewing tool kit (page 7)

Templates (page 124)

Pencil

¹/₂ yard (.5 m) of batting

³/₄ yard (.7 m) of muslin or other lining fabric

1 piece of cotton strapping, 2 x 38 inches (5.1 x 96.5 cm)

64 inches (162.6 cm) of drawstring cording

Safety pin

make

the patchwork exterior

1 For this bag, you will need to create three main quilted segments that have a wide main center fabric (in this case green): these segments will eventually become the left, bottom, and right sides of the bag. Cut these three center fabric pieces of varying widths, from 7 to 9 inches (17.8 to 22.9 cm). The length for all three pieces should be 17¹/₂ inches (44.5 cm).

2 Cut and sew strips of stash fabric on both sides of the three main green pieces.
To continue making each segment unique, the strips can vary from 1 to 4 inches (2.5 to 10.2 cm) in width **(fig. A)**. The length of the strips can vary also; some must be 17¹/₂ inches (44.5 cm) long, but others can be shorter. Place template A on the fabric to gauge the length and width of these outer strips.

3 Using template A and the patchwork pieces, cut out the three shapes **(fig. B)**. Mark all single and double notches.

4 Using the patchwork pieces as a template, cut three pieces of batting.

fig. A

fig. B

fig. C

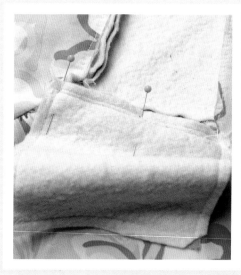

fig. D

fig. E

5 Layer each patchwork piece with a piece of batting, and pin and stitch along the outside edges.

6 Machine quilt the layers together along the seam lines.

7 With right sides together, line up two of the quilted segments, aligning the notches. Double pin at the single notches; you will not sew between the double pins. Sew together using a ¼-inch (6 mm) seam allowance.

8 Repeat step 7 in like fashion to attach the third quilted segment **(fig. C)**.

9 Cut two pieces of coordinating fabric and two pieces of batting that each measure 4 x 4 inches (10.2 x 10.2 cm). Layer each fabric square with a batting square and stitch the layers together around the outside edge.

10 With right sides together, pin the prepared fabric square to the center segments. Be sure to double pin at the single notch marks as a reminder to stop sewing at the notch marks. Begin to stitch at the single notch, leaving ¼ inch (6 mm) unstitched on both sides of the square **(fig. D)**.

11 Repeat step 10 in like fashion for the other two sides, but stitch all the way up and beyond the last single notch at the purse opening. Turn the patchwork piece right side out and press the seam allowance open **(fig. E)**. Repeat this process for the other side of the bag.

the lining

12 Using template A and muslin (or other lining fabric), cut three pieces for the lining. Mark all single and double notches and stitch them together as directed in step 7.

13 Cut two pieces of coordinating fabric that measure 4 x 4 inches (10.2 x 10.2 cm).

14 With right sides together, pin the small fabric squares to the center segments. Be sure to double pin at the single notch marks as a reminder to stop sewing at the notch marks. Begin to stitch at the single notch, leaving ¼ inch (6 mm) unstitched on both sides of the square.

15 Repeat step 14 in like fashion for all the sides, but stitch all the way up and beyond the last single notch at the purse opening **(fig. F)**. Press the seams.

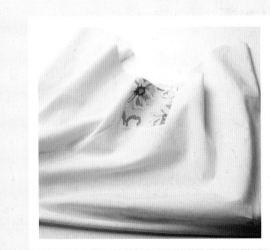

fig. F

the loops & strap

⑯ Prepare the cotton strapping by cutting a strip of the main fabric that measures 1¹⁄₄ x 38 inches (3.2 x 96.5 cm). Center the strip on the strapping, turn the fabric edges under ¹⁄₄ inch (6 mm), and use a zigzag stitch to secure. The cotton strapping used here is 2 x 38 inches (5.1 x 96.5 cm), but you can use strapping with a different width. Set aside.

⑰ With the main fabric, cut a strip that measures 2 x 36 inches (5.1 x 91.4 cm). Press the strip in half lengthwise, and then press the raw edges under ¹⁄₄ inch (6 mm). Stitch closed.

⑱ Cut the stitched strip into twelve 3-inch (7.6 cm) segments. Fold the segments into loops, and then pin and baste them at the bag's opening, with six loops on the front and six on the back.

⑲ With right sides together, place the outer bag into the lining. Pin the top edges **(fig. G)**.

⑳ At the strap openings fold and pin the lining ¹⁄₄ inch (6 mm) toward the wrong side on both ends.

㉑ Sew the outer and lining bags together, making sure to start and stop at the strap openings for both sides. Snip the angles and clip corners.

㉒ Turn the bag inside out through a strap opening. This process can be tricky as the bag is fairly large and the opening is fairly small.

㉓ Sew a basting stitch at the strap openings, on just the outside panels. Gather the baste stitch.

㉔ With right sides together, pin the prepared strap to the outer bag at the double notches, and stitch across **(fig. H)**.

㉕ Take a tuck in the lining and hand stitch down **(fig. I)**. If your strap is wider, you may not need to take a tuck.

㉖ From one of the coordinating fabrics, cut a strip that measures the circumference of your cording plus ³⁄₄ inch (8.3 cm) wide and 64 inches (162.6 cm) long. Fold the fabric in half lengthwise with right sides together and stitch along the cut edge with a ¹⁄₄-inch (6 mm) seam allowance. Turn the casing right side out, and use a safety pin to pull the cording through the casing. Turn in the ends of the casing and stitch in place, catching the cord in the seam.

㉗ Thread the drawstring cording through the loops and tie.

fig. G

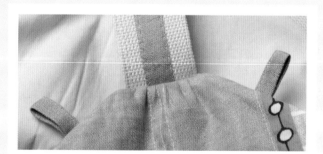

fig. H

fig. I

hip HEADBAND

Grab some scraps and get started! If you work fast, you can whip one up in every color.

from your stash

1 piece of main fabric (for base of headband), 10 x 10 inches (25.4 x 25.4 cm)

Fabric scraps (light and dark coordinating colors)

1 piece of fabric for the elastic casing, 10 x 10 inches (25.4 x 25.4 cm)

gather

Basic sewing tool kit (page 7)

Templates (page 123)

1 piece of muslin, 4 x 14 inches (10.2 x 35.6 cm)

Spray adhesive

Safety pin

11 inches (27.9 cm) of elastic, 1/4 inch (6 mm) wide

Embroidery floss

3 wood beads

fig. A

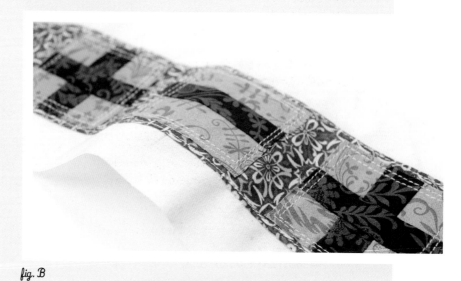

fig. B

fig. C

make

the headband face

1 Trace template A onto the piece of muslin following the straight grain of the fabric. Do not cut the muslin. Using the same template and the main fabric, cut a piece of fabric on the bias. Cutting this piece on the bias will prevent the finished piece from fraying.

2 Apply spray adhesive to the back side of the main fabric piece and position on top of the traced muslin piece.

3 Use the following measurements to cut the fabric needed to make two "plus sign" blocks:
- Eight 1 x 1-inch (2.5 x 2.5 cm) squares in light colored fabric
- Four 1 x 1-inch (2.5 x 2.5 cm) squares in dark colored fabric
- Two 1 x 2¹⁄₈-inch (2.5 x 5.4 cm) strips in dark colored fabric

4 Line up the squares in two rows of three—light, dark, light. Stitch the squares together in rows. Place a dark colored strip horizontally between the rows, building a plus sign block. Stitch the two rows to the fabric strip. Press the seams toward the dark fabric. Repeat to make a second plus sign block **(fig. A)**.

5 Use the following measurements to cut the fabric needed to make one "minus sign" block:
- Two 1 x 2¹⁄₈-inch (2.5 x 5.4 cm) strips in light colored fabric
- One 1 x 2¹⁄₈-inch (2.5 x 5.4 cm) strip in dark colored fabric

6 Line up the strips horizontally—light, dark, light. Stitch together the strips and press the seams toward the dark fabric **(fig. A)**.

7 Apply spray adhesive to the wrong sides of the blocks and position them onto the piece of main fabric.

8 Topstitch around each block and along the edges of the main fabric **(fig. B)**.

9 Trim away the muslin from the main fabric to define the shape of the headband.

the casing & elastic

10 Cut the fabric for the elastic casing on the bias, strip-piecing as necessary to make a strip that measures 1 x 20 inches (2.5 x 50.8 cm). Fold the casing strip in half and stitch it closed along the cut edge.

11 Using a safety pin, thread an 11-inch (27.9 cm) piece of elastic through the casing. Scrunch the casing so that the elastic sticks out from the ends **(fig. C)**.

12 Machine stitch both ends of the casing, catching the elastic in the stitches. This will make sure that the elastic stays in place.

13 Hand stitch the casing onto the headband.

finishing

14 Using the embroidery floss, add a decorative whipstitch along the edge of the headband. Hand stitch the wood beads to the center of each block **(fig. D)**.

fig. D

templates

Template B

clothespin caddy
(enlarge 400%)

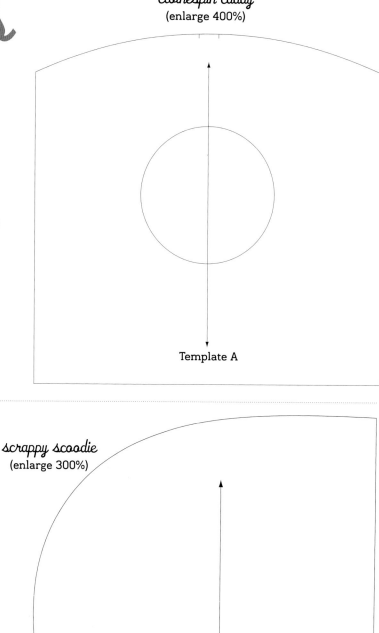

Template A

nesting bowl
(enlarge 200%)

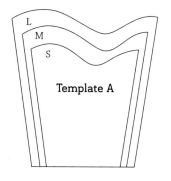

L
M
S

Template A

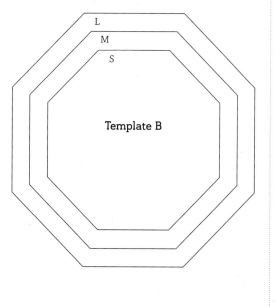

L
M
S

Template B

scrappy scoodie
(enlarge 300%)

Template A

cut 4 total

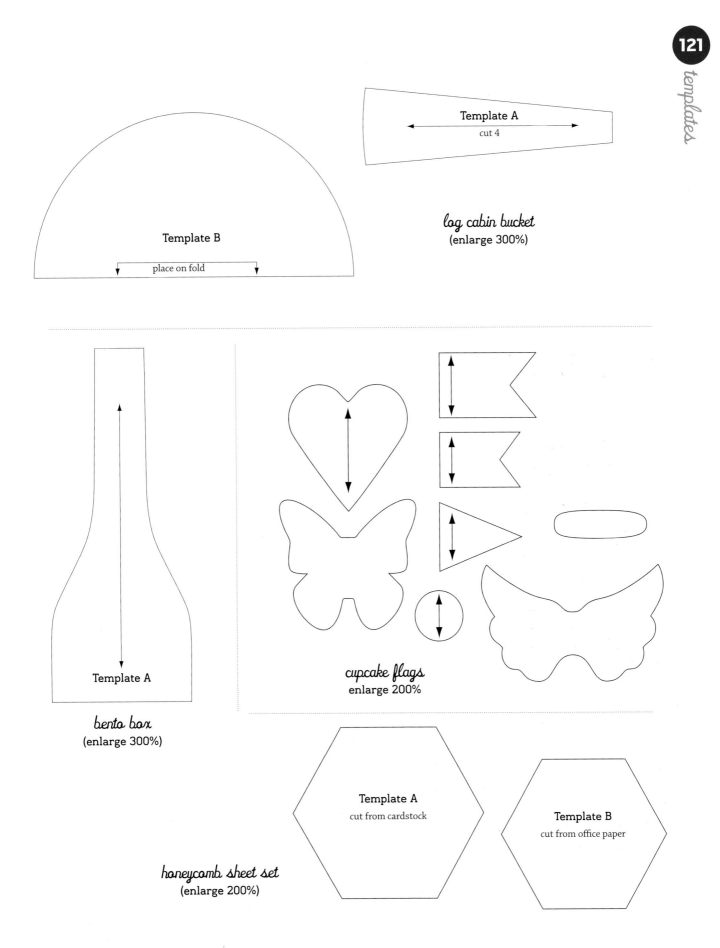

Template A
cut 4

Template B
place on fold

log cabin bucket
(enlarge 300%)

Template A

bento box
(enlarge 300%)

cupcake flags
enlarge 200%

Template A
cut from cardstock

Template B
cut from office paper

honeycomb sheet set
(enlarge 200%)

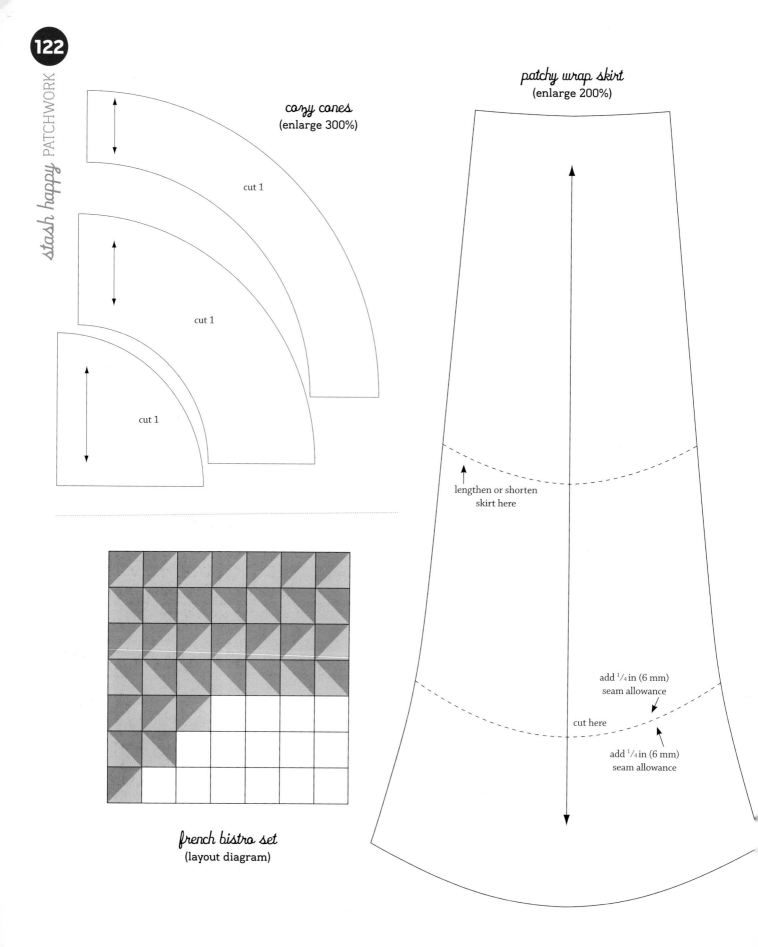

cozy cones
(enlarge 300%)

cut 1

cut 1

cut 1

patchy wrap skirt
(enlarge 200%)

lengthen or shorten
skirt here

add ¹/₄ in (6 mm)
seam allowance

cut here

add ¹/₄ in (6 mm)
seam allowance

french bistro set
(layout diagram)

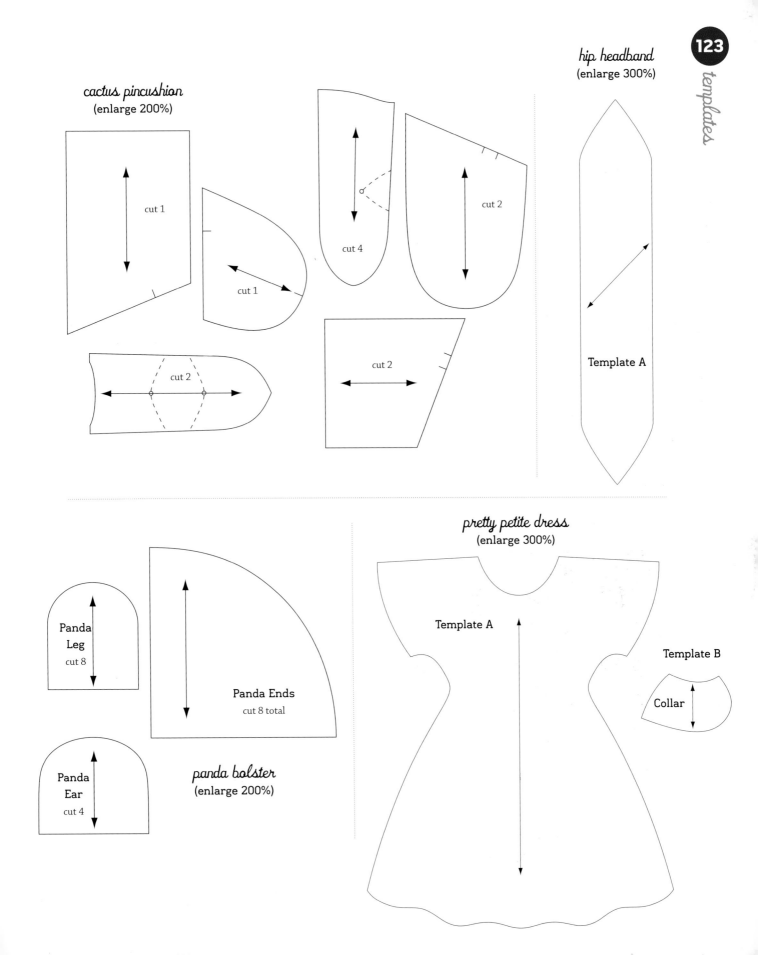

hip headband
(enlarge 300%)

Template A

cactus pincushion
(enlarge 200%)

cut 1

cut 1

cut 4

cut 2

cut 2

cut 2

Panda
Leg
cut 8

Panda Ends
cut 8 total

Panda
Ear
cut 4

panda bolster
(enlarge 200%)

pretty petite dress
(enlarge 300%)

Template A

Template B

Collar

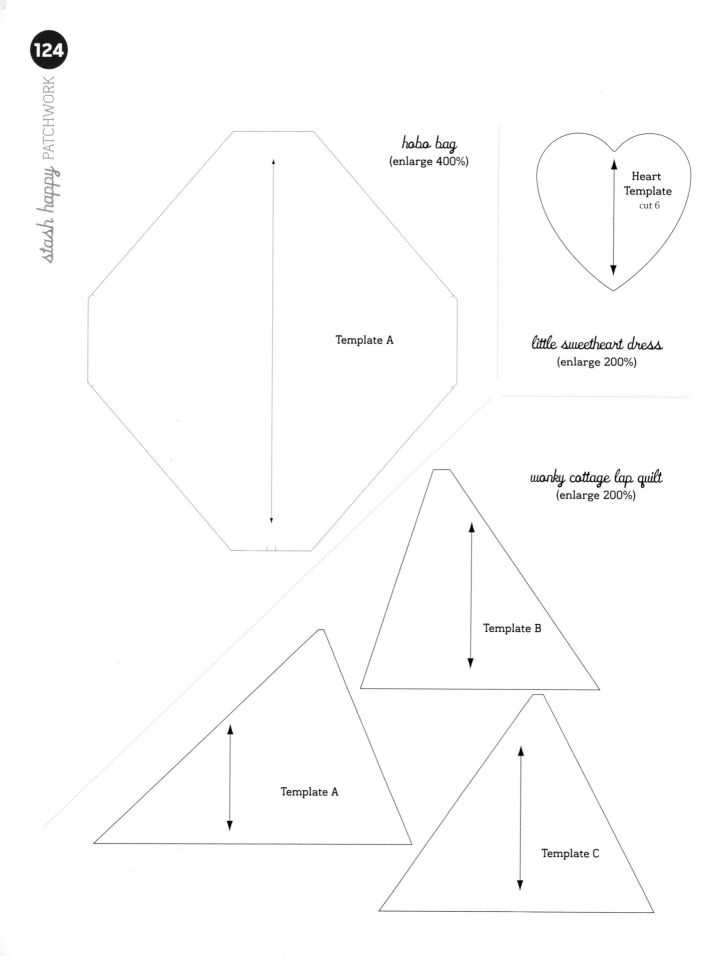

hobo bag
(enlarge 400%)

Template A

Heart
Template
cut 6

little sweetheart dress
(enlarge 200%)

wonky cottage lap quilt
(enlarge 200%)

Template B

Template A

Template C

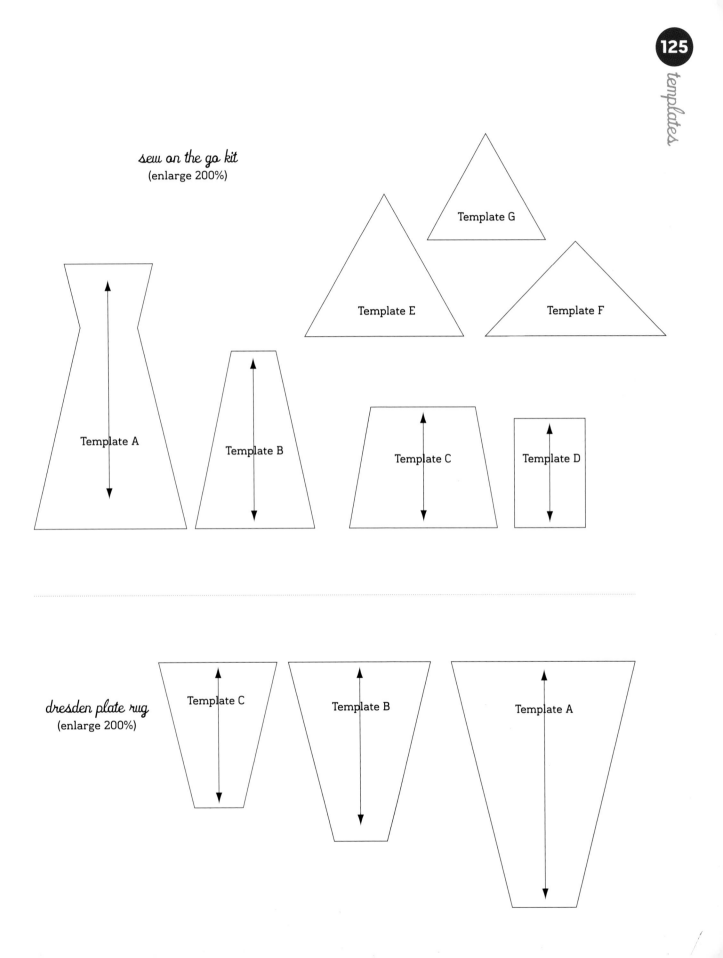

sew on the go kit
(enlarge 200%)

Template A

Template B

Template C

Template D

Template E

Template F

Template G

dresden plate rug
(enlarge 200%)

Template C

Template B

Template A

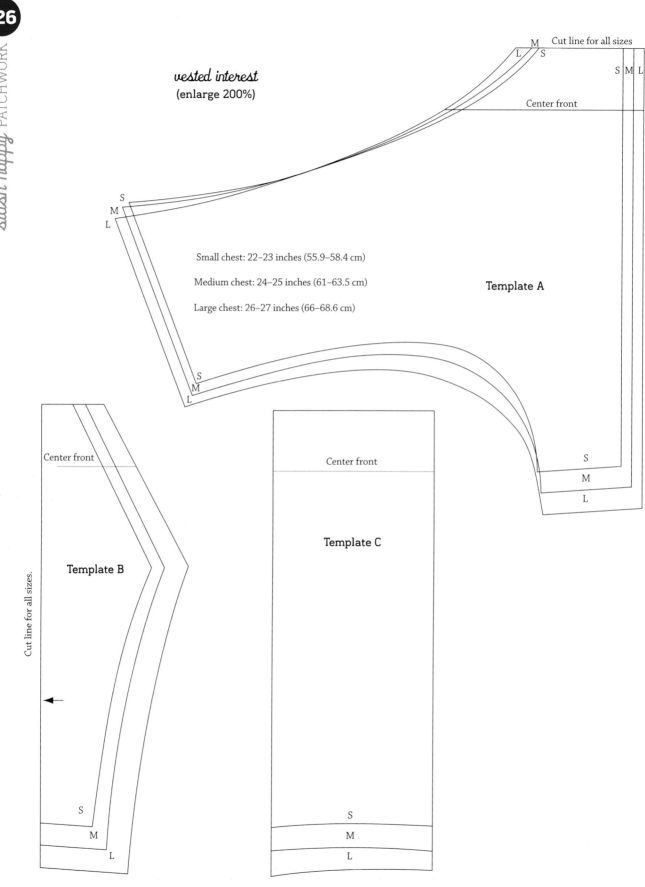

vested interest
(enlarge 200%)

Cut line for all sizes

Center front

Small chest: 22–23 inches (55.9–58.4 cm)

Medium chest: 24–25 inches (61–63.5 cm)

Large chest: 26–27 inches (66–68.6 cm)

Template A

Template B

Center front

Cut line for all sizes.

Template C

Center front

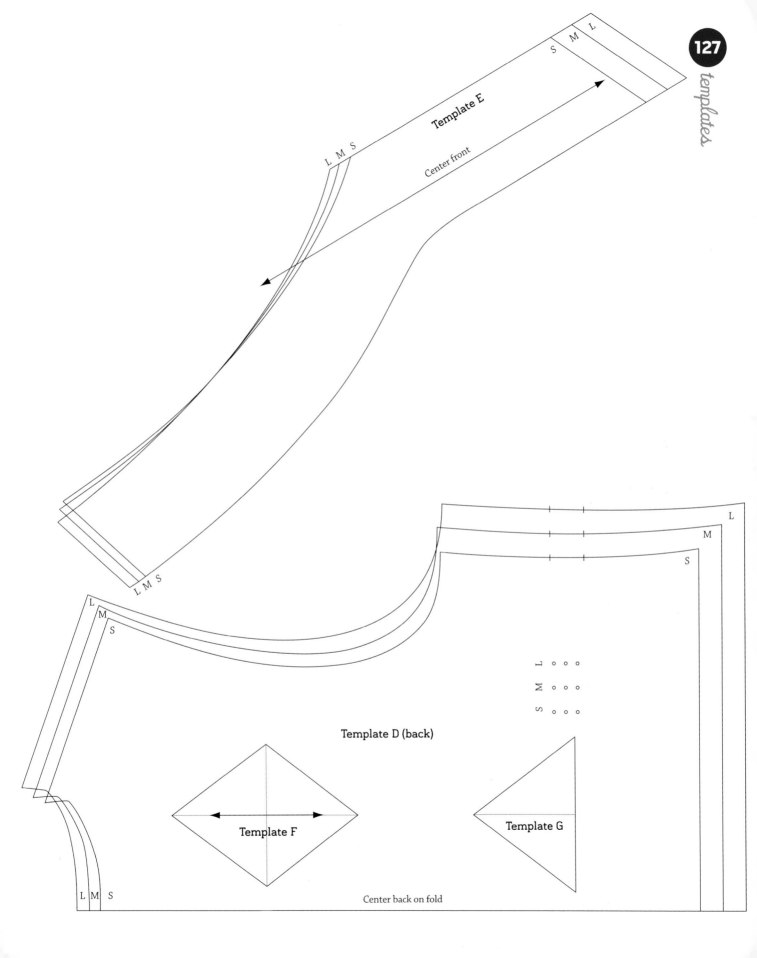

Template E

Center front

L M S

S M L

L M S

L
M
S

S M L

L
M
S

S ○ ○ ○
M ○ ○ ○
L ○ ○ ○

Template D (back)

Template F

Template G

L M S

Center back on fold

about the author

Cynthia Shaffer is a quilter and creative sewer whose love of fabric can be traced back to childhood. At the age of 6, she learned to sew and in no time was designing and sewing clothing for herself and others. After earning a degree in textiles from California State University, Long Beach, Cynthia worked for 10 years as the owner of a company that specialized in the design and manufacture of sportswear. Numerous books and magazines have featured Cynthia's work. She lives with her husband, Scott, sons Corry and Cameron, and beloved dogs Harper and Berklee in Southern California. For more information visit her online at www.cynthiashaffer.com.

acknowledgments

I'd like to thank the entire Lark Crafts family for believing in me and in this book. In particular, I am grateful to Amanda Carestio for her guidance and patience throughout the process. Also, many thanks to the good people at Moda Fabrics and Westminster Fibers for their support. Throughout my entire life, my mother has encouraged me to do what I love, for which I am ever grateful. To my family— Scott, Corry, and Cameron—thank you for allowing me the space and time to focus on this project and for offering honest input and feedback that helped me work hard to get things just right. And finally to my friend and colleague, Jenny Doh— thank you for listening, imagining, and being with me to make it happen.

I'd also like to thank the following models: Gwendolyn Alvarado, Cecilia Hernandez, Emily Jansen, and Jeremie Perez.

index